ORGANIZING
AGAINST
CRIME

Redeveloping the Neighborhood

Crime and Delinquency Series

Reference Group Theory and Delinquency
R.E. Clark, Ph.D.

Paroled but Not Free
R.J. Erikson, M.A.

Resocialization: An American Experiment
D.B. Kennedy, Ph.D. and A. Kerber, Ph.D.

The Prevention of Crime
S. Palmer, Ph.D.

Straight Talk from Prison
L. Torok

Organizing Against Crime
A. Sorrentino

ORGANIZING
AGAINST
CRIME

Redeveloping the Neighborhood

by
Anthony Sorrentino

HUMAN SCIENCES PRESS
Formerly *BEHAVIORAL PUBLICATIONS INC.*
72 FIFTH AVENUE, NEW YORK, N.Y. 10011 (212) 243-6000

Library of Congress Catalog Number 76-21840

ISBN: 0-87705-301-4

Copyright © 1977 by Human Sciences Press
72 Fifth Avenue, New York, New York 10011

Printed in the United States of America
789   987654321

Library of Congress Cataloging in Publication Data

Sorrentino, Anthony.
  Organizing against crime.

  (Crime & delinquency)
  Bibliography: p.
  Includes index.
  1. Juvenile delinquency—Illinois—Chicago—Prevention.   2. Crime prevention—Illinois—Chicago—Citizen
participation.   I. Title.
HV9106.C4S57   364.4'09773'11   76-21840

To My Wife and Children

CONTENTS

PART III.   THE NEIGHBORHOOD AND THE CITY

INTRODUCTION*

Chicago, home of some of the world's biggest criminals, has also been where some of the world's best criminologists have worked. But while the former, from Al Capone to the Blackstone Rangers, have been highly visible to the public, the criminologist's audience has been much smaller, more academic than public; this in spite of the enormous interest Americans have in crime and our belief, though often skeptical, that knowledge—or science, at any rate—is power, and necessary to an educated public in a democracy.

The newspapers daily stun us with lists of casualties and dismay us with investigative reporting on the administration of criminal justice. Although many of these presen-

*For support which made this essay possible, I wish to acknowledge the Institute for Juvenile Research in Chicago and the Center for Research in Criminal Justice, University of Illinois at Chicago Circle; especially Joseph Puntil of the institute and Hans Mattick of the center. My thanks go also to Helen MacGill Hughes, Florence Scala, Solomon Kobrin, and James F. Short, Jr.

9

tations of specific crimes and abuses run circles around the more plodding inquiries of the social sciences, we receive from the news media no systematic exposition on any topic concerning crime. Instead we are confronted with a series of ephemeral spectacles. One month a prisoner furlough program hits the headlines, next month the injustices in juvenile justice are spotlighted; plea-bargaining becomes the outrage, then the inefficiency of the courts is exposed —and after a period long enough to make it news again, we hear once more about furloughs. Perhaps this craze for novelty and for "fighting a war against crime" rather than affirming better, lasting values is itself a cause of crime.

It is currently a commonplace that citizens must get involved in the fight against crime, but the indignation and fear of the citizen are impotent unless they are accompanied by information about everything from door locks to courts and prisons—and, more important, by expanded insights such as criminologists should provide.

This book provides one such insight. It is a vivid description of a method of preventing juvenile delinquency. Of course, not all crime is committed by persons under 17 years of age; not even all delinquency is crime (for example, truancy, running away from home). But much crime is committed nowadays by juveniles,[1] and some individuals declared delinquent (though a minority) continue into adult criminal careers—partly as a result of being labeled delinquent. Attention is crucial here also because it is generally easier to change the habits of youths than of adults or at least to avoid reinforcing habits that bring pain and even ruin to the lives of both victims and offenders.

Where should we direct our efforts to prevent delinquency? For the Chicago Area Project the locus of the problem has been in the social situations where a child develops, especially the whole immediate neighborhood where the child lives. The problem itself is seen as social

disorganization, including the inability of adults to commu-
nicate conventional values to their children. The solution
is to help organize the residents of a neighborhood into a
community, and the essence of this program is for the
residents themselves, with indigenous leadership, to take
the initiative in solving their own problems, which
strengthens their sense of responsibility; and to take credit
for their accomplishments, which strengthens their sense
of pride. This process itself creates a more ordered moral
climate, which reduces a child's chance of becoming delinquent.

.This book narrates one of the programs of the Chicago
Area Project, located on the Near West Side of Chicago,
primarily when it was a slum inhabited by Italian immigrants, an area of high rates of delinquency. Since delinquency is viewed here in a broad social context, the book
takes up several other problems: ethnic identity, the aliena-
tion of the school from the community, work with adult
offenders, urban renewal, and so forth. The Near West
Side, turf of Al Capone, Jane Addams, and Mother Cabrini,
America's first saint, has always fascinated the public, and
this book tells about it from the inside—from the viewpoint
of an Italian immigrant in Chicago during the 1920s.[2]

But sociological study of delinquency? Participation of
residents in community problem-solving? What's new
about that? When the theory which guides the Chicago
Area Project was formulated in the 1920s and applied to
area projects in the 1930s, both the theoretical and practical moves were highly innovative. One reason they seem
commonplace today is precisely because of the influence of
the Area Project. This is not well known to the public because the founders of the movement were academic men
who did not seek popular acclaim, who concentrated their
efforts in local areas rather than using the news media to
fight a city or statewide system, as is fashionable today, who
yielded the spotlight to local leaders and published books

on the sociological theory behind the Area Project rather than on the experiences of applying that theory.

Narratives of action would have been most appropriate by indigenous leaders and workers in the slum, but these people were usually not very literate, although they were more effective with their audience than college graduates would have been. A handful of academic and journalistic articles have appeared about the Chicago Area Project, but, except for a limited-circulation volume,[3] this is the first book published about it. James Short has said, "The full story of the Chicago Area Project has never been told, and it may now be beyond recapture."[4] This book salvages a part of the full story from oblivion and may stimulate the production of a more complete account. It can also give ammunition to critics, for, as Jon Snodgrass has pointed out, while the sociological theory behind it has undergone various methodological examinations, the Chicago Area Project itself has not had a thorough critique—or, by the same token, a thorough defense.[5]

For if the techniques of the Chicago Area Project seem commonplace today, they also seem outmoded. Now problems are inevitably translated into political terms, and dealing with the problem of delinquency on the local level appears outrageously inadequate. We are told to fight concentrations of power that transcend but are the ultimate, real causes of the slum or the ghetto and therefore of crime and delinquency. In light of the charges that it is superfluous and wrongheaded, does the Chicago Area Project have any important unique contribution to make today?

Yes, it does. First, there is reason to believe that interpretations of crime and delinquency by political activists, even if true theoretically, are often inadequate in practice: for example, when preoccupation with a distant revolution results in the neglect of more immediate problems the resolution of which could crucially improve the lives of some individuals. Saul Alinsky, perhaps the most influential recent American pioneer in political activism, was a worker for the Chicago Area Project from 1931 to 1940, frequently on the Near West Side. His work with the Area Project was the source of his tactic of citizen participation, though he always represented it as his own invention with antecedents in the democratic ethos. The hyperbole in Alinsky's 1945 book *Reveille for Radicals* is justified by his hope that by fighting one can change the establishment; conflict strategy *was* his own invention. But in 1976 a judgment is possible not on his words but on his deeds.

Alinsky helped found The Woodlawn Organization (TWO) on Chicago's South Side in the early 1960s. It was based on his model of conflict by the powerless with the powerful who were the source of ghetto conditions. However, in 1973 John Hall Fish wrote:

> TWO, although successful in building an organization, was unable to address some of the systematic causes of the social problems Woodlawn faced. On a week-by-week basis TWO was most successful in what might be termed little issues that affected a relatively small number of people and could be pursued to a successful outcome with relatively meager organizational resources. A boy was kicked out of school, a woman was cheated by a merchant, a slumlord turned off the heat. These were bread-and-butter issues that helped build the organization.
>
> The desired outcome is a "we-did-it" attitude where the emphasis is as much on the corporateness of the "we" as on the accomplishment of the "did-it."[6]

This creating of community consciousness by solving neighborhood problems primarily on the local level is essentially what the Chicago Area Project has been doing for over 40 years. Anyway, is there any reason why the social and the political models cannot coexist?

Second, if the Area Project outlook is widespread today, why concern ourselves with this book except as a curious history? There is reason to believe that social interpretations of crime and delinquency are never so firmly established that they cannot be forgotten—or never learned by people who revere data but ignore history— then rediscovered as if they were new. (A can-opener sits there—you would be foolish to invent one—but an old idea reappears ...) A "General Memorandum—Correctional Outcome Project" from the School of Social Service Administration at the University of Chicago (p. 2) states:

> Corrections and other social services have long operated to too great a degree on the assumption that problems in social functioning demand only attempts to promote change within the individual. In reality, helping demands that major attention be given to the individual's immediate environment, as well.

This is not dated 1929, as it might be, but January 9, 1974. As for the modus operandi, every other report on this subject has something like the following: "We want to involve representatives of the local community in this departure from more traditional approaches to delinquency control."[7] Obviously this corner is never turned once and for all, and the Chicago Area Project has a continuing mission of keeping this model in view, an end toward which this book is a means.

The Chicago Area Project has a future. What about its past? Its origin cannot be fully described apart from the historical sequence in which it arose. The last hundred years have seen a series of "new criminologies." The most innovative and influential criminological work in the late nineteenth century was done by physical anthropologists; in the early twentieth century, by psychologists and psychiatrists; from the 1920s to 1950s, by sociologists; and nowadays, by lawyers or professors in centers of research in criminal justice, often connected with law schools.

20006328

Modern criminology began with the work of the Italian doctor Cesare Lombroso (1835–1909), and Lombroso got started during his postmortem examination of the famous brigand Vilella. On the interior of the lower back part of the skull he found a depression also found in inferior animals. Lombroso describes the "eureka" event:

> This was not merely an idea, but a revelation. At the sight of that skull, I seemed to see all of a sudden, lighted up as a vast plain under a flaming sky, the problem of the nature of the criminal—an atavistic being who reproduces in his person the ferocious instincts of primitive humanity and the inferior animals. Thus were explained anatomically the enormous jaws, high cheek-bones, prominent superciliary arches, solitary lines in the palms, extreme size of the orbits, handle-shaped or sessile ears found in criminals, savages, and apes, insensibility to pain, extremely acute sight, tattooing, excessive idleness, love of orgies, and the irresistible craving for evil for its own sake, the desire not only to extinguish life in the victim, but to mutilate the corpse, tear its flesh, and drink its blood.[8]

Lombroso was one of those extremely influential thinkers who appear from time to time in the history of ideas. From him came not only the notion of the "born criminal," a throwback to an earlier stage of evolution—after all, Darwin was in the air—but also the problem of the insanity of genius, which is even today often considered to be a problem. Followers of Lombroso alleged a variety of physical stigmata of criminality and published photographs of men with wild looks, doubtless resulting from the deprivations of jail and the explosion of the photographer's light powder. However, it must be said in favor of Lombroso that he directed attention to a study of the individual offender—before him the study of legal principles had been the fashion (as in Cesare Beccaria's *On Crimes and Punishments*)—even if he began with what was in a way the most obvious thing, the individual's body.

Meanwhile another tributary was starting to flow into the mainstream of this history. One of the first settlement houses in the United States had been set up on Chicago's Near West Side in 1889 by Jane Addams, out of the objective necessity of helping the urban immigrant poor and the subjective necessity of giving the first generation of college-educated American women something to do.[9] Since they were women, one thing the male establishment allowed them to do was to concern themselves with children.[10] They noticed that children were sent to the same courts and jails as adults, but they were often just released because judges could not bear to send them to adult jails, and they would reappear in various courts throughout the city because there was no central record kept on them. The ladies of Hull House got the first juvenile court in the world started in 1899 across the street from Hull House. Once children "in trouble" were appearing in one place, it became obvious that no one knew why they were there or what would be best to do with them. Again the "child-savers," especially Julia Lathrop and Ethel Dummer, acted. In 1909 a clinic was established adjacent to the juvenile court to study and treat delinquents. By thus formulating a practical and theoretical concept, *delinquency* was invented, as surely as was the electric light bulb.

Surely the child-savers were motivated by the most benevolent feelings, but today they are criticized most severely for setting up a structure of personalized treatment for children that routinely violates their rights as citizens. Patrick Murphy has pointed out that the immigrant parents whose children appeared in the juvenile court in its early days "often could not supervise these urchins because they were employed in nineteenth-century sweat shops, working long hours at low wages for the same families who produced the leading reformers attempting to save the children from their horrendous existence."[11] A good example of Murphy's point is Sara L. Hart, who was related to the Hart of Hart, Shaffner and Marx and participated in the child-saving movement at Hull House.[12]

The founder and first director of the world's first "child guidance clinic" was William Healy (1869–1963). Healy, an immigrant from England, had been helped to attend Harvard College by people at a Chicago bank where he had been an office boy. He later took a medical degree and practiced for a few years. Healy had been a student of William James's at Harvard, and when Julia Lathrop consulted James about who would make a good director, James recommended "the good doctor," as Snodgrass calls him. Healy began with a *tabula rasa,* except for the Lombrosian model and his own medical skills, but the latter soon canceled out the former; in his medical examinations Healy could find none of the Lombrosian criminal stigmata on the children whom the court referred to him. Healy was interested in Freud, and his assumption in the early days was that delinquency was a result of emotional pathology; the first name of the clinic was "The Juvenile Psychopathic Institute," and one of the techniques of treatment was the "talking cure." Eventually Healy realized that the medical model could not account for all cases of delinquency, and he developed a pluralistic method of studying the physical and personality characteristics of individuals, a method he put forth in his magnum opus *The Individual Delinquent* (1915). Later the name of the clinic was changed to the Institute for Juvenile Research (IJR). It is still involved in psychological services and research.

Yet another tributary of the history was forming at the University of Chicago; founded in 1892, it included the world's first sociology department. Unlike nineteenth-century scholars who had mainly theorized about social problems, the teachers of sociology at the University of Chicago emphasized the importance of actual participation in the social situations a student intended to write about. Shortly after Clifford Shaw (1895–1957) became a graduate student there in 1919, he began to acquire practical experience as a probation officer for the juvenile court. In 1926 he was chosen to head a new department of sociology at the Institute for Juvenile Research. Early in 1927, Henry McKay (born 1899), another former sociology graduate student at the University of Chicago, joined Shaw as his assistant.

Although Healy, who had left IJR by then, had begun to recognize the importance of social situations in the etiology of delinquency, for him this was only an aspect of personality development, not a field to be systematically explored in itself. Therefore the intellectual circumstances in which Shaw began his work included a remnant of the Lombrosian notions, a somewhat more pronounced concept of delinquency as mental illness, and the predominant paradigm of dealing with the personality problems of individual delinquents. At the outset of his first major publication, Shaw wrote:

> Although the individual delinquent has been studied intensively from the standpoint of psychological tests, biometric measurements, and emotional conditionings, comparatively little systematic effort has been made to study delinquency from the point of view of its relation to the social situation in which it occurs. The present volume is limited to a study of the geographic distribution of school truants, juvenile delinquents, and adult offenders in the city of Chicago and represents an initial phase of a situational approach to the study of delinquency.[13]

There had grown up at the University of Chicago sociology department a vision of the city as an organism, and the first step in Shaw's inquiry was to locate those areas of the city that had high rates of delinquency. (Shaw is often criticized today, even by the current IJR sociology research staff, for not realizing that those rates of apprehended delinquency reflect processes of selection by the police; but he was quite aware of this, claiming that "there is no evidence to show that the children living in areas of low rates are involved in such serious behavior difficulties as larceny of automobiles, hold-up with a gun, burglary, and the like.")[14] The second step was to study those areas intensively for factors related to delinquent behavior. According to Shaw, any study of delinquent behavior must take into account the character of the community in which the behavior arises. The present volume describes the features of one typical "delinquency area."

These areas were found to be located adjacent to industry; they had been formed when industry had expanded into the area and landlords had failed to make improvements in residences in expectation of further industrial expansion. No matter what immigrant group—German, Irish, Jewish, Italian—had moved through the area, high rates of crime and delinquency had persisted. The racial hypothesis of the natural inferiority (the "born criminality") of one or another group was replaced by the area hypothesis to explain high rates of delinquency for those groups: each group as it entered America sought the cheapest housing and was thus forced to enter an area with an already entrenched tradition of delinquency, which the group about to leave the slum transmitted to the newcomer. The old-world values of the parents were not communicated to their children, who were attracted by new-world adventures. Delinquency is then regarded as the manner in which the delinquent achieves for himself those human satisfactions which are presumably wished by members of all social classes. As each group improved its economic status and moved away from the slum, rates of delinquency for that group went down.

Shaw and his associates (McKay being the most important) published six books. Three were primarily autobiographies of delinquents that concretely presented the conditions in which juvenile offenders lived: *The Jack-Roller* (1930), *The Natural History of a Delinquent Career* (1931), and *Brothers in Crime* (1938). One amassed data to support their interpretations: *Juvenile Delinquency and Urban Areas* (1942, rev. ed. 1969). Two publications did not have a wide public distribution, though they may have been more influential than the others: *Delinquency Areas* (1929) and *Report on the Causes of Crime: Volume II: Social Factors in Juvenile Delinquency* (1931). The last of these was part of Number 13 of the Wickersham Report, famous for its investigation of Prohibition. McKay also contributed to the President's Commission on Law Enforcement and Administration of Justice in the late 1960s.

Shaw's publications presented new facts to academic and professional people, and to an extent to the public as well. But it is unlikely that one will study crime and not be led to some form of overt action, and the appropriate response to community disorganization as a cause of crime is to organize communities. With the help of Ernest Burgess, a professor of sociology at the University of Chicago, Clifford Shaw established the Chicago Area Project. Around 1930, programs were getting started in three areas of Chicago that traditionally had high rates of delinquency: South Chicago (around the steel mills), the Near North Side, and the Near West Side (both adjacent to the central business district of the city). Just as the theoretical opponent had been the psychological approach to the delinquent, the practical opponent was the social worker, who, like the missionary, entered a community to "help" but who did not believe community residents themselves had the intelligence or will to take any responsibility or initiative. Resources under the control of a downtown office were doled out in the slum, but the poor had no participation in the process.

Perhaps the best metaphor to describe Shaw's operation is the delivery of a speech. The conventional agency worker at that time (and how often today!) approached his audience with a prepared text, which he read to them as if giving orders. Shaw, on the other hand, began with an examination of his audience, whom he could then approach with a repertory of useful topics or techniques to the end that they would be able to speak for themselves. The most important of these techniques was to find people who were already in one way or another leaders in the community— in other words, speakers whom the audience trusted—indigenous leaders who would also be acceptable models for action: "The former leader of the shoplifting ring automatically became leader of the new club by virture of her natural leadership qualities."[15] "It was the Chicago Area Project that first carried out such activity on a systematic and sustained basis."[16] The Chicago Area Project "became the prototype for delinquency prevention and welfare programs of the Kennedy-Johnson era."[17] However, publicity and credit to the Area Project have apparently never been widespread: "In 1937, the United States Housing Act was passed. . . . The standards of the Federal Administration were high. But it never occurred to anybody that the people might make their own decisions about playgrounds, housing design, or management policies. So the institutions became more and more institutionalized."[18]

The Chicago Area Project was incorporated in 1934. It consisted of a staff of community organizers on the payroll of the Institute for Juvenile Research, then part of the Illinois Department of Public Welfare; these workers helped indigenous leaders in an area develop an organization in the manner described in this book. A board of directors primarily of businessmen from throughout the city acquired funds to dispense to various community committees to pay for programs the residents themselves decided on; otherwise the board had (and still has) no decision-making role. In 1957 the sociological research staff at the Institute for Juvenile Research, which is now part of the Department of Mental Health, split off from the community services function, which first became part of the Illinois Youth Commission, then part of the Illinois Department of Corrections. On January 1, 1976, the state-supported staff of community workers became part of an independent delinquency prevention commission of the state of Illinois. In the early 1970s, to qualify for private funding, a person not on the state payroll became executive director of the Area Project. The author of this book was director of the Area Project after Shaw's death and is executive director of the new state commission.

Lest the official history obscure the feeling tone of the movement, this must be said about Clifford Shaw:

> Rather than founding a spiritual movement, as he might have done in an earlier age, he abandoned Christianity, borrowed many of its principles and values, and attempted methodically to create a community reform movement ostensibly based on science. One early worker has remarked that in the enthusiasm of the early days, many felt as acolytes, zealously hoping to kindle a popular return to hamlets and ethical humanism within the confines of the city. Shaw was an apostle of community organization as a way of saving the American city from its inherently great capacity for generating physical deterioration and social disorganization.[19]

Shaw created a unique amalgam of academic, government, and business people, community residents and leaders, and criminal offenders. During most of the 1930s Saul Alinsky worked for Clifford Shaw at the Institute for Juvenile Research and the Chicago Area Project. One of his tasks was to collect life histories of juvenile delinquents. Many of these life histories (now at the Chicago Historical Society) mention Alinsky with great kindness. Apparently

Shaw and Alinsky intended to co-author a book from this material that was to be called *Companions in Crime*. But Alinsky's mind was elsewhere:

> As a kid was telling me of an A & P store he robbed and another of a gas station he heisted, Hitler and Mussolini were robbing whole countries and killing whole peoples. I found it difficult to listen to small-time confessions. Most of my time was spent in anti-fascist and CIO activities.[20]

When Alinsky left Shaw in January 1940 to set up his own organization, the Industrial Areas Foundation, he carried with him both theoretical and practical parts of the Chicago Area Project ideology:

> The opening of the door on the study of crime confronts one with a broad vista of social disorganization. Such aspects of this dreary scene as unemployment, undernourishment, disease, deterioration, demoralization, and many others, including crime itself, are simply parts of the whole picture.[21]
>
> The secret of the Back-of-the-Yards Council—and all the other organizations I worked at since—was: The people weren't fronting for anyone. It was *their own* program.[22]

In *Reveille for Radicals* Alinsky wrote at length about "indigenous leaders," as Shaw had spoken about them before him. Alinsky never mentioned Shaw in print, however. Surely the Shaw-Alinsky relationship would make an interesting study.

Saul Alinsky had been an improverished student at the Oriental Institute of the University of Chicago, when, according to him, the president of the university, Robert Maynard Hutchins, offered him a fellowship in criminology.[23] (Alinsky is most likely mistaken: only department chairmen offered scholarships.) Consequently Alinsky was not committed to the dominant paradigm in criminology. His personal political interests motivated him to develop a new model, the unique feature of which was to locate the ultimate causes of community disorganization in structures of economic and political power outside the community: "The life of each neighborhood is to a major extent shaped by forces which far transcend the local scene."[24] The strategy of change is then to do battle with those transcendental forces:

> If we free ourselves of the schackles of wordiness, the statement of purpose is clear and simple: the job is the unslumming of the slum. This means the battling of all those forces in the city and the nation which converge to create the human junkyard—worse, the cesspool—known as the slum.[25]

To do this required the organizer to act as "an abrasive agent to rub raw the resentments of the people of the community; to fan the latent hostilities of many of the people to a point of overt expression."[26]

Shaw located the cause of delinquency in social conflicts, and he cooperated with business and government to bring resources to the community. Even though there is some evidence that he acknowledged the culpability of industry, he apparently believed that he could get more out of them by persuasion than by opposition. Alinsky, standing on Shaw's shoulders, located the causes of those social conditions in the powerlessness of the people, whose task was then to generate conflicts with power. At the same time, sociological theory concerning delinquency in the 1950s and 1960s typically began with a consideration of Shaw and McKay, but formulated a conception of delinquency causation based on the economic desires which all Americans share and the illegitimate means the economically deprived must employ to satisfy those desires. Short has said: "The foundations laid by Shaw, McKay, and others not only have stood the test of time but remain of vital significance for contemporary research and theory and for programs oriented to delinquency control."[27]

However, the dominant paradigm in criminology today is certainly economic and political—in the Chicago media today "CAP" stands for Citizens Action Program, a citywide organization of citizens who conduct campaigns against abuses by government and industry—and its application to delinquency is seen nowhere more clearly than in agitation to change the juvenile court. In *Our Kindly Parent . . . The State,* Patrick Murphy says: "We termed our practice Alinsky law—using a variety of legal actions (some valid, some spurious), investigations, and intelligent use of the media to try to move, embarass, and change bureaucracies."[28]

These efforts in the juvenile court have been brilliant,[29] but there is growing awareness that other parts of radical programs, such as talk about "ultimate causes," in fact overlook or even delay possible valuable action, in the same way as psychoanalysis deals with ultimate causes but may accomplish less in years than a crucial conversation with a friend does in a day. Norval Morris has said:

> In a sense, the radical utopian position, arguing that it is ingenuous to try to improve prisons, damning all reformist efforts, and insisting that we concentrate only on the restructuring of society required for social equity, is the ultimate "cop-out." It is an abnegation of responsibility.[30]

While scholars and senators formulate new delinquency prevention programs,[31] the Chicago Area Project persists with its 43-year history of theory and experience. Connected with state government, assisted by business and industry, nevertheless its leaders see their beginning and end in developing autonomy in the people of a community. The program is persistently opposed by state administrators, who, in the manner of the agencies the Area Project has always fought, would prefer to keep a tighter hand on "their" resources: thus the Area Project is not without its own conflicts with the establishment, fought from within. The belief of many people is that the Chicago Area Project "continues to show undiminished vigor, continued development in its own right, and the experience continues to be useful and relevant."[32] Today 18 community committees operate in Chicago; in addition, there are over 40 other groups in suburban Cook County and probably over 100 groups throughout the state which are organized on the model of the Area Project.

The parts of this book reflect stages in the history given above. Part I presents the life of an individual, especially early emotions in a psychological mode. Part II gives a sociological view of the problems of a community committee. Part III takes up some political problems of the community and the organization. The tone of the writing changes from the intimately personal in the first section, to a narrative of actions in the second, to an official chronicle of events in the third.

The last section of the book deals with internal structures and difficulties of the Near West Side Community Committee and the Chicago Area Project today and gives a glimpse of connections with city, state, and national problems and powers. Chapter 8 gives the history of efforts by residents of the Near West Side to renew their own neighborhood; the narrative flows along with every indication that the future is open. Then Mayor Daley appears with "his" university, and we stroll right off the cliff. This was one of the earliest and most infamous urban renewal projects,[33] and the history of early citizen participation has never before been told so fully as it is here.

In many ways, though, the meat of this book is in its first part, consisting of two chapters: "Growing Up in Little Italy," and "Inferiority and Enthusiasm." To begin with, this is a life history, a fragment of an autobiography. (Sorrentino has identified his career so completely with Shaw and the Chicago Area Project that one may claim that the rest of the book, though it does not focus on him, is indeed his autobiography.) Life histories in criminology also have a history. While Lombroso was measuring skulls, Henry Mayhew, the multi-talented founder of *Punch,* was roaming the streets of London collecting information concerning *London Labour and the London Poor* (1862), including "those that will not work" (volume 4)—prostitutes, thieves, swindlers, and beggers. Mayhew published many of these eloquent interviews, somewhat in the manner of Studs Terkel today. William Healy invented the practice of asking the children he studied to relate their "own story," an essential part of the data he collected. Clifford Shaw, following the precedent of W. I. Thomas and Florian Znaniecki's *The Polish Peasant in Europe and America* (1918), used life histories to illustrate the area hypothesis of delinquency causation. Life histories were extremely popular in sociology and in society generally between the two world wars,[34] though sociology abandoned them when it turned theoretical in the late 1940s.[35] At Shaw's urging that he write his life history, Sorrentino wrote an initial draft of this book in about 1950, when the earlier events were fresher on his mind than they would be today, and it has now been brought up to date.

Shaw, McKay, and other leaders in sociology wrote sociological theory but did not write their autobiographies.[36] Instead they encouraged delinquents they met to write their life histories. This book is a personal document that assimilates the two: it is by a man who, having engaged in delinquent behavior as a boy, came to be a leader of a movement to prevent delinquency. As such it provides a view of the world of a "delinquency area" as well as of an individual's motives to change both himself and that area. This is an insider's view of a movement that held that action and speech about that action should come from within

individuals in a community and be directed toward changing conditions inside that community.

Italian immigrants came to America searching for a
new world, but they found an old world, an already established social system made up of earlier immigrants defend-
ing their own gains. Sorrentino's early life is the story of a
boy moving into that old world, which for him, a youth, was
new. It is easy to discover from his example the elements
of any such movement: an intense motive, in this case feelings of inferiority and optimism; a "guide," here a man who
encouraged him by giving him responsibilities he carried
out; friends, who saw the world as he did and were perhaps
a little further along than he was; books, which acquainted
him vicariously with a world he wished actually to enter;
and a problem, the vast contradiction between the slum he
lived in and the downtown business district he worked in.[37]

If the tone of this story smacks too much of Horatio
Alger for today's readers, it is probably because of the
bouyancy and adventure expressed here and in many of the
life histories collected by the Institute for Juvenile Research from Italian delinquents on the Near West Side in
the 1920s and 1930s. This adventurousness is much rarer
in America today, especially in the experience of the group
that has replaced European immigrants as the conspicuous
population of juvenile correctional institutions. Black delinquents speak of a gang organization conceived along
military lines, and their beginning in delinquency is likely
to have been recruitment by a gang, unheard of in the
earlier period. Sorrentino and his associates were encouraged by academic sociologists to realize the need for organization. Youths today, benefiting from the earlier work,
imbibe a concept of "the system" in their mother's milk,
but ironically, coming after the establishment is even more
firmly set, they have still more need for organization. However, the development from gangs to clubs today is similar
to what happened in the 1930s (see Chapter 5).[38]

It is difficult for us today to realize the enormous authoritarianism in 1920s America. Complaints against cold and aloof schoolteachers have now been replaced by complaints against "permissive" teachers. The Italian father, a patriarch thundering down commands of old-world good and evil, has been replaced by the black mother rapping to her children about making something or making nothing of their lives. The immigrant child's experience was an innovation over fixed, rigid norms from a rural culture that no longer applied in the fresh, open world of urban America, while the black child today typically must make his own values in a culture that provides little moral guidance and puts oppressive restraints on his obtaining the very materialistic values it so strongly advertises. Bootlegging has been replaced by the more deadly traffic in drugs.

Sorrentino begins this book by situating the Near West Side "within the shadow of the Loop." In 1930 that shadow was cast by the new 30-story Board of Trade building, topped by a benevolent Goddess of Corn gazing down. In 1976 the Loop is dominated by the 110-story Sears Tower, the world's tallest building, from the top of which nervously pulsates a strobe light. An organization such as the Chicago Area Project, that respects the powers of consent and growth in individuals and communities and prefers cooperation to a strategy of conflict that may itself be oppressive is not out of place in the world today; it needs to be rediscovered.

JAMES R. BENNETT, PH. D.

ACKNOWLEDGMENTS

I was inspired and encouraged to write this book over 20 years ago by the late Clifford R. Shaw while I was a staff member of the sociology department of the Institute for Juvenile Research and the Chicago Area Project. My training and experience in community organization was acquired at the institute, starting in 1934, when the first of three experimental programs for delinquency prevention was launched jointly with the Area Project.

In addition to Clifford Shaw I am particularly grateful to Henry D. McKay, retired research sociologist at the institute, for his guidance, intellectual support, and friendship over a period of more than four decades.

For the actual publication of this book, I am profoundly grateful to James Bennett, who saw merit in the first rough draft of the manuscript, encouraged me to bring it up to date, and then graciously volunteered to edit the manuscript and write an illuminating introduction. Without his labor, support, and dedication, this finished product would not have resulted.

My deep appreciation also goes to several persons who read the manuscript and made valuable suggestions: Helen MacGill Hughes, Cambridge, Mass.; Professor Irving Spergel, University of Chicago; Dr. James McKeowan, University of Wisconsin (formerly DePaul University); Mike Townsend, assistant professor, Sangamon State University; Joseph Puntil and Emil Peluso, Institute for Juvenile Research; Aurelia Tornabene and Erwin W. Pollack, teachers from the William H. Ray Elementary School; Len Hilts, a professional writer; Reverend Paul Asciola, National Center for Urban Ethnic Affairs, and Joseph Italiano, a teacher from Australia.

I also want to pay tribute to other co-workers at the institute who made available documents from which I profited in writing Chapters 5, 7, 8, and 9. In addition to Henry McKay, these persons included Solomon Kobrin, Harold Finestone, and James F. MacDonald. Other staff members who read the manuscript and offered encouragement and suggestions include Joseph Giunta, Russell F. Anderson, George Parsons, Daniel D. Brindisi, and Ray Raymond. I also am in debt to the late Paul D'Arco and to James Serpe for the use of their diaries in writing Chapter 4.

I am also grateful to the many persons who supported the Chicago Area Project, both on the Near West Side and throughout the city: Peter R. Scalise, Elliott Donnelley, William C. Douglas, Ralph E. Williams, Carroll H. Sudler, Sr., John P. Wilson, Jr., Daniel P. Haerther, Julian Schwartz, and William H. Wethers III. My sincere thanks also goes to the entire board of directors of the Chicago Area Project and the institute's child guidance associates for their assistance toward publication. In addition, I wish to thank Helen Prendergast, not only for typing and secretarial services but for her interest and support throughout my career.

Finally, I am deeply grateful to the many volunteers who gave of their time, talents, and money to develop and promote this enterprise. And above all I am grateful to those persons who must remain anonymous, for their cooperation in relating to me their life experiences which are described in this book.

My final tribute: I dedicate this book with love and gratitude to my wife Ann and children—Robert, Patricia, and Dolores—as a very small expression of the thankfulness I feel and owe them for their patience, tolerance, and understanding during the 40 years I was working in the neighborhoods and involved in civic projects and in the administrative operations described in this story.

Part I

THE BOY AND THE WORLD

There was a child went forth every day;
And the first object he look'd upon, that object he became;
and that object became part of him for a day, or a
   certain part of the day, or for many years, or
   stretching cycles of years.

Walt Whitman

Chapter 1

GROWING UP IN LITTLE ITALY

DISCOVERING AMERICA

Within the shadow of the Loop just west of the Chicago River is the Near West Side. Jane Addams did her pioneer work in this area; Al Capone got started here, too. It was in what was then the heart of this district that, legend has it, Mrs. O'Leary's cow kicked over the lantern that started the Great Chicago Fire. During the Roaring Twenties our community achieved the zenith of its notoriety and was dubbed the "Bloody Twentieth" (that is, the Twentieth Ward—now part of the First Ward) by newspapers.

On the other hand, many civic enterprises originated here that later achieved national recognition. University students and social workers gathering material on "how the other half lives" made social surveys and investigated social problems, and for many years the area attracted visitors on sightseeing tours.

This is where I arrived with my family at the age of six, a small immigrant boy who could not speak English, and I remained in and around the Near West Side of Chicago for almost 40 years. One of my problems was the task of learning to live in a new country, but in many other respects my difficulties were typical of what almost every boy who lives in a poor, deteriorated community confronts.

I remember it was a cold day in 1919 when I entered this strange new land, this huge metropolis with its somber atmosphere and peculiar traffic noises. We seemed to be Lilliputians in the land of the giants. The never ending stream of cars, trucks and horse-drawn wagons and teams on the main streets seemed like demons of death in contrast to the tranquility of the scene of our home in Sicily, dominated by the Mediterranean.

With us was nostalgia for our native land and uncertainty about the future. My mother would look out from our dingy flat to the drab streets and cry for "Marsala Bella." Our loneliness lasted some months, but gradually we began to experience some joys and good fortune and became better accustomed to our new way of life. We realized that this new land had many things to attract us.

The innumerable shops and stores displayed a great variety of foods, packages of candies and sweets, gay and colorful boxes, cans, and appliances. All were available— for all to see, if not to have—in practically every neighborhood store. From that moment on I have never ceased to marvel at the abundance of food and goods available in this country.

Like many, if not most, of the immigrants who have come here, we settled for a short time at the home of relatives. After we landed at Ellis island in New York, we spent the first week with my father's brother in Brooklyn. My uncle Pietro wanted us to stay there, but my father, who was a man of his word, had promised his brother Carlo that we were going to Chicago. When we arrived in Chicago we lived with my uncle Carlo. We had only one small bedroom for the whole family. In addition to my parents, my family consisted of Nancy, an older sister, and James, a younger brother. My father contrived to allot each of us sufficient space on the one bed to give us a relatively restful night.

My father joined his brother in a candy factory, and my mother went to work with my aunt in a tailor shop. My sister, then nine years old, functioned for a time as the mother of the house and ministered to our needs in our parents' absence. Our aunt warned us to remain indoors and admonished us not to open the door to strangers. When the representative from the gas company called to read the meter—an entirely unknown contrivance to us— we unwittingly created a neighborhood furor. The man knocked and knocked on the door until finally three neighbors, led by a kindly old lady, came to our door and persuaded us in familiar Italian voices to open the door.

After that it was comforting to know that Mrs. Panico would be there if other strangers intruded. I recall that in those early days we were often apprehensive when we were left alone, listening to sounds totally unfamiliar to us. Intermittently throughout the day, peddlers in horse-drawn wagons hawked their wares in tones which often seemed garbled to us. In the distance a peddler mournfully chanted, "Rags a line" (rags and old iron). The fruit and vegetable peddlers were a familiar sight; they were also common in Sicily. Totally unfamiliar to us were the exciting noises of the horse-drawn fire engines galloping through the streets. (I believe they were converted to motor vehicles around 1920).

But perhaps the most depressing, almost sickening sound we heard was the funeral march played by an Italian band that accompanied the hearses. The mournful music had a melancholy and depressing effect on us. Incidentally, the trumpet player of this band was Louis Panico, the landlady's son, who shortly after became the leader of his own band. A few years later his very popular orchestra played in nightclubs, and he became known as the "king of the Wabash Blues."

Another street sound we became acquainted with in those early days and which continued right through the Depression was the coal peddler. In those days virtually every home was heated with coal, ordered by the ton. However, some families used up the supply before they had enough money to reorder in quantity. In the interim they would purchase coal from the peddler, usually three bushels for a dollar.

After listening to the sounds of peddlers, fire engines, and funeral marches during the day, we were delighted with the return of our parents. My father always brought home candy, and my mother usually brought home groceries and bakery goods.

After living with my uncle and aunt for six months my parents were able to save a little money, and they rented a flat nearby on Aberdeen and Harrison streets. From this moment on we made regular visits to the 12th Street Department Store (owned by Phillip & Son, but referred to as "Filliposon") to purchase furniture and household goods, all on the monthly installment plan. Unlike in Italy, material desires in America could be gratified instantly, a few dollars down and the balance a few dollars a week or monthly. One of the big purchases, I remember, was the Victor Victrola, where we played records by Caruso and other famous singers. For laughter and hilarity, we played Italian records by "Nofrio," a Sicilian comedian. His anecdotes and stories usually dealt with the everyday problems of living and with the frustrations of an Italian trying to express himself as he struggled to speak English—when he tried to use the telephone (there were no dial telephones in those days), to order a meal in a restaurant, or purchase special articles in stores.

One of the humorous stories I recall is about the immigrant who learned to say "appla pie and cuppa coffee." But after ordering the same thing day after day, he got tried of this diet. He asked a friend who was more knowledgable, and he taught him to say "hamma sandwich." Proud of his expanding English, he went to the restaurant and ordered, whereupon the waiter asked, "White or rye?" Confused, the immigrant rattled, "Appla pie and cuppa coffee." This delightful ethnic humor, unhappily, has disappeared.

The other major diversion was visiting friends and relatives. In addition to my uncle and aunt, who were childless, there were many *paesani* from Marsala who frequently came to our house—with, of course, reciprocal visits. Here the adults conversed at length about their families and experiences in Sicily while drinking wine or eating homemade cakes and pastries and sipping anisette, strega, and other Italian liqueurs. The folktales they narrated, both humorous and serious, were entertaining and instructive. They also had proverbs for every occasion. I have long since forgotten most of them, but somehow a few on money matters stick in my mind. *"Sensa soldi non se canta la messa,"* they would say, meaning the Mass is not said without payment, or the priest will not say the Mass without money. On the glittering effect of money they would say, *"E sordi fanno veri vista al orbi,"* money will make even the blind man see.

The conversation at other times was on the somber, mystical side. There were sometimes references to the *malocchio,* the evil eye; if a person had a persistent headache and was listless, it was suspected that someone had given him the evil eye. To deal with the phenomenon there was a method of both prevention and treatment; my mother would go around sewing or tying pieces of red ribbon or cloth on our garments, or she would make the "horns," with her fingers. If a person appeared to be suffering from the *malocchio,* then the treatment consisted of a ritual of *preghiere,* prayers, which usually some old lady was especially versed in performing. If the old lady began to get tired and started to yawn, this was a sign that the person had actually been afflicted with *malocchio*. After a few minutes both the old lady and the patient would begin to feel normal and return to their duties as though nothing had happened. Then there were the "worms." Here again special prayers were said by the old lady, who crossed your forehead or stomach with olive oil. Oftentimes a person so treated was reported to be miraculously cured.

My father was well liked and respected by the *paesani*. As the oldest son of a large family he was considered a leader, and hence members of the family or relatives asked for his advice or his mediation of family disputes. He was regarded as fair in his judgments, and his character was held to be of unquestioned integrity. He sought to instill these same qualities in our family and often spoke of the importance of honesty and maintaining a good name. His guiding principles for family living were obedience, loyalty, love, respect, and honorable actions at all times.

I recall a lesson he taught me on the importance of respect. When entering the home we children were expected to acknowledge our father by obediently saying, *"Vossia me bene deca"* (give me your blessing); we were to address all of our elders in this manner. After a few years in America, I was beginning to think this was old-fashioned, and one day I refused to say it. Firmly and sternly my father ordered me out the door, telling me to come back when I was prepared to enter like a Christian. Somewhat rebellious, I entered again but stubbornly refused to utter the acceptable words. Again I was whisked out the door. Finally, after I had virtually frozen myself on the outdoor porch, I meekly re-entered and dutifully, but sotte voce said, *"Vossia mi bene deca."* My father responded, *"Dio ti benedice"* (God will bless you).

This sounds as though my father were religious, but he was not. Like many Sicilians in those days, my parents were only nominal Catholics. However, they adhered to many of the religious rituals, paying devotion to special saints and remembering their birthdays. A story was told that my father once prayed to St. Nicholas for the job he was seeking on his first trip to America a few years before we arrived. One day, after a fruitless search in Detroit, he came home worn out and frozen. He was so mad at St. Nicholas for not answering his prayers that he took the statue of the saint out on the back porch and said, "Now it's your turn to freeze."

While my father was a man of vigor and vitality, my mother was docile, had little initiative, and gradually became virtually dependent. Except for working during the first year of our arrival in Chicago, she was always confined to the house and local neighborhood; she never did learn to speak English. She died at the age of 76.

With the beginning of the new year, we were told that my sister and I had to go to school. My brother, who was not of school age, was boarded during school hours at the home of a distant relative. Most children from very poor homes, especially from immigrant families, are not ready for school, their first great experience outside the family. They are not emotionally prepared with assurances, explanations, and the introductions to some of the elementary tools of learning which children usually receive from middle-class families. Besides this lack, my sister and I were confronted with an even greater barrier in our old-world cultural traits and language. No friendly voice put us at ease. Fear and misery clutched us and remained within us for a long time. I'm not sure whether the bruising effect this had on our personalities has ever really healed.

The huge school buildings, the regimented appearance of things in the school, the tall, rigid-looking teachers who flaunted authority and exuded a pungent odor of powder and perfume—this was a strange, disturbing world. The principal was a tall middle-aged man, well fed, with a serious frown on his face and a stern, glassy look in his large eyes, which seemed out of focus. I thought of him as

the dominant ruler of the institution who meted out pun-
ishment to transgressors, not as a kind human being whom
I could like.

This setting inhibited me. I realized all too soon that
my Italian lingo and Italian-made garments set me apart
from the other children. This feeling of being different and
peculiar in the eyes of others further contributed to what
sociologist Robert E. Park refers to as "that sickening sense
of inferiority." There were constant reminders of this.
"Dago, dago, eats nothing but potatoes," the boys would
sing, with threatening gestures.

I reacted with some fear and a feeling that to strike
back would be futile, so for the time being I retreated and
sought a friendly response in a different way. For one thing,
I tried to be "good" in the classroom in hopes that I would
be rewarded with the approving glances of the teacher. But
deep within I had the feeling that this was going to be a
rough world, that I was going to be pushed around and
dealt with by hostile forces which my child's mind could
then little understand. I now believe these new pressures
had a profound effect upon my childhood personality.

Thus, rather early I had experiences in the competitive
struggle for power and status which so clearly characterizes
American society. It was clear to me that there were only
two alternatives: to withdraw and be satisfied with my meager lot or struggle to achieve some of the good things in
life. Somehow, as we shall see later, the experiences that
followed enabled me to pursue the latter course of action.

Working, Playing and Death

In Europe boys are encouraged to learn a trade while they
are still children and are often apprenticed by the time they
are in their early teens. In keeping with this tradition my
father thought it was time for me, when I was barely ten

years old, to begin to learn a trade. One day after school he took me to Mr. Briatta's barbershop and arranged for me to report there every day after school. My duties were twofold: pay close attention to the way Mr. Briatta and his assistant cut hair, shaved faces, and trimmed moustaches; secondly, keep the floor swept and the cuspidors clean. But no pay.

I was constantly distracted from these tonsorial endeavors by Mr. Briatta's enormous red moustache. I swear it was a foot long, and he wore it as proud as a peacock, often twirling it with his fingers. Besides, the boys would beckon me to go out and play marbles or pitch pennies. After a few weeks my father inquired about my progress, and Mr. Briatta told him rather sadly, by stroking his chin with his knuckles (a gesture which literally means no, it can't be done—impossible) that this boy is not cut out to be a barber. Thus ended my shortlived apprenticeship.

Another early work experience my father arranged was working with our landlord's family when we moved to Polk Street. Mr. DeGiovanni was a shoemaker and had a repair shop on the ground floor. The family lived in a rear apartment, where his wife and about six children assembled men's and women's garters. The two oldest boys would go to A. Stein & Company, a few blocks away, every week with their homemade push wagon to pick up the rubber and metal parts, which had to be assembled by hand. Then all week the children, in their spare time, worked around a huge kitchen table, making garters. I helped out for a season in this friendly sweatshop after school, and each Sunday I was rewarded with one whole quarter.

Shortly after, we moved a few blocks away across from the DeLeo Bakery, and on certain days I would accompany the driver as he delivered bread to homes and stores all over the city.

Whatever ambitions I may have entertained to become a sailor or captain of a ship in Sicily were abandoned. I wanted to do what other kids did, such as belong to a neighborhood gang. I set forth meekly at first, making friends with kids on my block, and gradually I became accepted as part of the neighborhood gang. Before long I was playing peg and stick, marbles, and baseball.

Our gang would make "bomb-fires," as we used to call them, and roast potatoes when the flames receded. Sometimes we would steal a bushel of coal from the coal peddler. Almost always we stole the lumber to make the fires. It was a fascinating game to jump over fences into somebody's yard for a prize box or bushel. Occasionally the butcher's chicken coop served as fuel. And if the boxes or crates were unavailable, you could always tear off a couple of pieces of lumber from somebody's fence. We'd fight with an enemy gang, breaking into their clubroom and ransacking the place as a way of getting revenge. Sneaking into a movie theater unnoticed by the vigilant ushers was a thrilling experience; our crowning achievement was when we sneaked into the gallery of the Old Star and Garter Burlesque House on Madison and Halsted. On a more regular basis, however, we went to the Waverly and Halsted moviehouses, where for 5¢ we could see Tom Mix, Hoot Gibson, Harry Carey, and other silent movie cowboy stars of that era.

Our small gang usually played in the streets, alleys, or backyards. An old basement or coalshed refurnished by our talents would constitute our clubroom. Sometimes the clubroom would be built on empty lots by the boys with boards acquired by devious means. An old kerosene lamp or stove furnished a little heat to thaw out the place. The clubroom was usually full of smoke, damp and smelly, but it was adventure. It was here that life took on meaning and we satisfied our desire for companionship. Although several settlements and centers were just a few blocks away, we did not attend them regularly—except for holidays, when free candy and apples were handed out.

One place I also attended occasionally was the old Jewish People's Institute—we called it the "Hebrew Institute"—where you could see movies for a penny and take out books at the branch library. I believe this was the beginning of my habit of picking up books and hence eventually to my hobby of collecting books. The JPI was located on Taylor and Lytle streets; by about 1925, when the Jewish population moved out, it was abandoned, and a few years later it was torn down. This is now the site of the Jane Addams Housing Project.

The little gang and the meager clubroom were the dominant influences in shaping our personalities. The settlements and community centers did good work, but the fact was that the rank-and-file kids of my neighborhood went there only occasionally. They played basketball and ping-pong and made handicraft articles, but the time spent on them was infinitesimal compared with the hours spent on the streets and alleys in random "unsupervised" activities, that were always stimulating and attractive.

Getting into mischief and taking things was a means of attracting attention and having new experiences. At times it was the only means of getting money for candy and movies. I remember my experiences with two brothers whose father, a drunkard, did not provide them with the little money boys need for childish pleasures. Consequently they got into the habit of begging along Halsted Street. I often went with them. I can see us now, dirty, raggedy little kids, pathetically pleading, "Mister, gotta pennie, please?"

After begging for pennies, I got to be a professional beggar of United Cigar Store coupons. The premium store where the coupons were traded was nearby, and I was attracted like a magnet to the pocketknives, flashlights, sleds, and rollerskates on display. I would find out the number of coupons required for each article, then begin earning them by going to a United Cigar Store, where I'd wait outside for the customer to come out and beg him for the coupons. It would take many months to accumulate enough.

We lived a block from a cookie factory, and on certain days when the wind was blowing our way the aroma of those freshly baked cookies made our mouths water. Responding to those delightful odors, we would saunter over to the cookie factory and ask the drivers if we could help them unload the wagons, so that they'd give us some of the cookies sometimes returned by the stores. But when the driver wasn't looking, we would snatch a box of fresh cookies and munch on them in our shanty club or hoard them for later on.

In our shanty club or on some of our excursions through alleys or empty lots, we would assert our manliness by picking up butts and smoking them. This was kids' play, an activity that did not make us feel particularly guilty—but even now, almost 50 years later, I recall with a sense of guilt one of those clandestine smoking parties that occurred in a different context.

It was at the time of my father's death. He was laid out in our home and a somber, soul-sickening atmosphere pervaded our dwelling. The strong odor of flowers, candles lit on each side of the casket, my mother and sister crying and pulling their hair hysterically, the neighbors and relatives who milled about the house with sorrowful expressions— this feeling of gloom, death, tragedy, and disaster which filled our home did great damage to me during those three days. It has continued to influence me even to this day. There I was, a small, scared, insignificant kid in that bleak, dreary, despairing situation, with a feeling in the pit of my stomach that my greatest treasure had been taken away, that my life had been crushed.

I suppose I could stand just so much. Every now and then I would go out and play with the other kids, trying to hide the great pain within by outwardly acting tough and hard: Oh well, it was just some kind of a big show they were having at the house. I joined the kids and put on a front—

acted as if the world were still the same. Alas, so did the other kids, for they soon pulled out a whole package of cigarettes and passed them around. Sure, I would take one and smoke it like a man! I did. And ever since I've wanted to hide and forget that incident, wanted to divulge it to no one.

But now that I am writing this book I'm telling about it, because one of my intentions is to try to understand myself by recalling my childhood—and, in the process, to understand children who are even today subjected to circumstances similar to what mine were. Now I can understand that my behavior was an innocent, childish whim, an outlet, an escape from the deadening weight of that situation which I could no longer withstand. Since then I have learned that a given act has a reason, a history. Children don't just suddenly act up; their behavior reflects the successive social experiences they have had in the family, play group, and neighborhood.

For a while I was a boy scout at a local settlement. This developed quite accidentally. A friend of mine interested me in scouting by explaining the wonders of camping and outdoor life. I joined the troop so I could have the kind of life I'd read about in the Rover Boys and Tom Swift series. It was one of several constructive experiences that enabled me to prepare myself for a better life.

It was a common activity for boys of ten or eleven years of age in my neighborhood to be shoeshine boys. I had mentioned the idea of being a shoeshine boy a number of times while my father was working, but he always reprimanded me for even considering it. Where he came from, he said, only the lowest characters would ever stoop to such a disgraceful occupation. The tradition of the small, enterprising businessman was strong in his mind. No son of his would ever be a bootblack.

One day when I was ten years old my father was brought home in a taxi from the candy factory. He had gotten the first of a series of paralytic strokes which, about

a year later, caused his death. While he was home con-
valescing from the first stroke I again proposed that I
become a shoeshine boy, but he still denied permission.
We were then living on a meager subsistence, advanced
from an insurance policy, of $1,000 from the candy firm he
worked for. The idea of drawing out more than a few hundred dollars haunted him: he knew he was going to die and
didn't want to leave us completely penniless. For a while he
gave himself courage and even contemplated opening a
fish store. But it was not to be.

Meanwhile, I saw other boys earning about $2 a day on
Saturday and Sunday by shining shoes. I realized that $4 a
week would be a great help to our slim family budget.
(Fortunately, at that time another uncle, a younger brother
of my father, had come to join us. He paid board, which
helped a great deal). The boys were telling me how easy it
was to shine shoes. One day I went along with a boy and
watched him as we walked around Madison and Halsted.
Inspired by this experience, I again approached my father.

I told him how simple it was. I even promised to carry
the shine box out of the neighborhood covered in a package so it would not reflect on him. Finally, when I realized
he said neither yes or no, a sign he was giving in, I set about
to raise $1.10 by selling homemade lemonade in the neigh-
borhood. This was more or less kids' play, but, penny by
penny, I raised the required amount to purchase the shoeshine box and thus embarked upon my career as a shoeshine boy.

When I got on Madison and Halsted—"hobo land" or
the "area of homeless men" or "skid row"—scores of shoeshine boys were busily at work. This was not encouraging.
How could a neophyte like me crash into this monopolized
market? Aimlessly I wandered off a few blocks north to the
Randolph Street wholesale fruit and vegetable market. By
about noon I surmised that the workers and proprietors of
the wholesale fruit and vegetable establishments might be

ready to go home, so naturally a shoeshine would interest them. It did, and by doing a good job I established a regular trade. After that I earned about two dollars every Saturday. On Sundays I covered the cheap hotels and lodging houses, can houses and taverns on West Madison Street.

The nickels and dimes jingling in my pockets were wonders. They gave me a sense of accomplishment at the end of the day and enabled me to purchase food and household requirements. Equally important, they enabled me to go to the movies to see cowboy pictures and buy candy and hot dogs along the way. After my father died, this small but regular financial help was more needed than ever before.

After two years as a roving shoeshine boy, I graduated into a shoeshine parlor. The Greek proprietor of a combination hat-cleaning, pressing, and shoeshining business called me in as I was passing with my shine box, and after demonstrating my ability—I naturally put on my best airs, cracking the cloths in rhythmic fashion and hurling two brushes confidently in my palm—I was offered the job. This meant working from 8 A.M. to 11 P.M. on Saturday and from 8 to 4 P.M. on Sunday, a total of 23 hours over the weekend. In addition to the shoeshining I had to scrub hats in benzine, wash the cuspidors, feed the pressing machine, and mop the floors. I worked side by side with Mexican and Negro men and earned about $6 every weekend.

After my father died, we were left without a breadwinner. I was 11 years old. My sister was 13 and still in grammar school. My uncle worked in the candy factory, but with his meager wages he could only pay his board and support his family in Sicily. Soon after this he returned to Italy to be reunited with his family. Since my father was not a citizen—he died five years after we were in this country—we were not eligible for any allotment from governmental agencies. To tide us over for a few months, some generous friends contributed some funds. But a regular income was needed, small as it might be. A neighbor suggested my sister could work in a paper box factory. Despite child labor laws, my sister went to work at the age of 13. With her $15 a week, plus my part-time work as a bootblack, we supported our family.

This was not a happy period. I sometimes wondered how we lived. Possibly the cementing force was the strong Sicilian sense of family. It was tough on my mother to be left without a man, but the thought of remarrying was simply outside her tradition. In the old-world Sicilian family, the widow wore black clothes for years, practiced denial, and stayed close to home. As a result my mother developed few outside interests, never learned English, and, I'm afraid, became self-centered as she grew older. In some respects, the situation was even more tragic for my sister, Nancy. She had to work long, monotonous hours in a nearby paper box factory, many days plagued with migraine headaches. After supper, she often had to sleep for several hours to recover from her weakened condition. She was the breadwinner and, in a sense, head of the household. She had my father's vigor and exuberance and tended to make the decisions. She used to adore my father, respected him fiercely, and all her life looked for a man with his qualities. Of course, she never found him. (Finally, disillusioned, she married when she was 39 years old and died when she was 49).

My sister and I especially resented the idea of "charity," though for a time after my father's death we had to accept it. This consisted merely of some staple commodities furnished by the county, some of which we could not use since we were not accustomed to such products, and occasionally clothing and a pair of shoes we detested wearing because of the inescapable "charity style" they had. After a few months of humiliating experiences with "charity," we worked hard and never again had to resort to this form of support.

My father's death when I was 11 had a shocking impact on me and my family. It created an indescribable void in our lives. We were left alone in the world. My shoeshine occupation then became an urgent necessity. In addition, on weekdays, I went junking with the other boys, through alleys, dirty yards, dilapidated buildings, factory districts, flophouse areas, where we could garner rags, bottles, or metals that we could sell for a few pennies. We found or "took" things wherever we could, occasionally jackrolling drunks along the alleys of West Madison Street. Fortunately, we were never caught.

STREET LIFE: VENDORS AND GANGSTERS

Speaking of junking reminds me of Felix, the junkman who lived next door to our house. He was a bachelor and lived alone in two dreary rooms lit with a kerosene lamp. He would set forth every day with his small pushcart to travel miles of streets and alleys in search of rags and metals. Returning at the end of the day with soot and dirt embedded on his lean but rugged face, he would sort out his junk in a shed in back of the house and store it until he had large quantities to sell. Day in and day out, year in and year out, Felix practiced his lowly art with never a variation in the humdrum routine. Being a next-door neighbor, I would frequently visit him as he returned with his junk at the end of the day and chat with him about his finds. If the finds for the day were scanty, it was quite apparent there would be no cheer in his voice. But perchance he had an abundant haul—then he would be more sprightly and eager to answer questions. He helped me and a pal of mine a great deal in our own junking endeavors.

On warm days after work Felix would sit in his yard alone with his corn pipe, and as he looked up in the sky I sometimes wondered was he thinking about a different, richer life? Or was he thinking of the countless alleys, of the garbage, dirt, filth, and rats which he came upon every day of his existence? Or was he, in his meditation, in his solitary, almost misanthropic role, at peace with the universe?

I recall, too, the time I used to go to Josie's grocery store down the block. One day as I entered the store, Josie, calm but quite concerned, pointed to a macaroni drawer where a mouse was playing havoc. "Please Tony," she said, handing me a rag, "catch it." With the dauntless spirit of a Sir Galahad I marched forth with the rag, pursued the mouse, and upon grabbing it squeezed it fiercely, squashing it to death. I don't care to remember whether the macroni I had previously purchased from Josie came from the same drawer.

Then there was Bozo, the umbrella man, drunk more often than not, who gruffly chanted, "Umbrella to repair" as he ambled along with his welding kit over his shoulder. We would taunt him, and he would threaten to hit us with his tools. "You're nothing but a drunken bozo," we would say jeeringly. On occasion he would be visited by an Irishwoman from the nearby rooming house district, and together they would get sickly drunk. Then he would chase her out and pull her by the hair as she fell off the sidewalk.

Besides the peddlers I have already mentioned, we had a number of other colorful itinerant vendors in those days. Of course the most common were the fruit and vegetable peddlers. They were also the most popular, since the Italians have a great passion for *fruita e verdura*.

When I was a child, we often had as a first course pasta —pasta and beans, pasta and cauliflower, pasta and broccoli, pasta and kohlrabi, pasta and lentils, pasta and zucchini with tomato sauce, and even pasta and peas. The regular spaghetti or linguini with meatballs or braccioli was reserved for Thursday and Sunday suppers. Because meat was scarce, these two days were designated for such dinners.

As we learned more about American food in later years, we would feel ashamed that we had been brought up on such peasant fare; but no longer. After decades of steaks and roast beef, and because being an ethnic today is becoming fashionable, we now again relish that wonderful peasant food. And Italian food is inexpensive and nutritious.

Pizza is of course very popular today. But I remember when it was sold on the street by our Neopolitan pizza man. On warm summer nights he would stroll through the streets with a large tub on his head, knife in hand, and with a musical chant announce, *"A pizza, calda, calda."* When a customer beckoned, he would ceremoniously place the tub on the sidewalk and cut the desired piece for 5 or 10¢, using the cover of the tub for cutting and his apron to wipe the knife. Not very sanitary, perhaps, but the aroma was terrific!

Another unusual vendor was the *passatempo* (pass time) vendor with his pushcart laden with lupini (a giant Italian bean treated in salt water), ceci, pumpkin seeds, and a dozen varieties of roast Italian beans. These tasty morsels were munched by the Italians as they sat in front of their houses on warm evenings. They added a glass of homemade wine. Another popular snack in our neighborhood was the five-cent "nuti sandwich," an earlier version of the hero or submarine sandwich. Actually, it often served as a meal, since it consisted of a large chunk of fresh Italian bread served with Italian cold cuts. When we did not go home for lunch during the school period, hundreds of kids would run to the Nuti bakery; but we were also influenced by that other famous sandwich, the hot dog. We had a vendor who made it seem imperative that you buy a hot dog, especially after a swim at the Sheridan Park Pool. *"Che mangia muore mai,"* Bruno would repeat endlessly (he who eats never dies), and besides, to add to its already tantalizing appeal, Bruno put in an Italian flourish—little hot peppers. Yes sir, he who eats never dies!

The Greek waffle man did not have a slogan, but when he came by in his colorful horse-drawn wagon, you ran in his direction for one of the most delicious treats of all. The wagon itself was a major attraction. It was one of a kind: high wheels, enclosed with windows, and gaily decorated with white, red, and blue colors. As you approached the wagon the Greek would flip a drop-down counter and fill your order. While he also sold hot peanuts and candies, the big seller was the hot waffles. As he proudly handed you a large piece for a few pennies, he would with a flourish sprinkle it liberally with powdered sugar. None of the present frozen variety will ever equal the delectable waffles of our now extinct waffle man.

In addition to the vendors there was always either a candy store or a grocery store with vegetables displayed on the sidewalks. All of these stores had some homemade lemonade, cold slices of watermelon, and some even had hot corn on the cob to eat right on the spot. These treats cost only a penny or two.

It was here on your street in front of your house where much of the drama of life was played. During the summer this was the important social center: everyone could see what was going on. Housewives would exchange news and confidences, watch religious processions, and deal with itinerant vendors.

Toward the eastern end of the Near West Side, around Halsted and Maxwell, was "the Market." Once the ghetto of Chicago, it became the marketplace for thousands of people, some who came from distant places, many of them formerly residents of this district who returned for bargains, which were to be had aplenty. Owned primarily by Jewish merchants, hundreds of stores and dingy stands sprawled along the sidewalks and streets, containing practically every known article to fill any human desire. The most motley assortment of wares could be purchased there— clothing, hardware, furniture, fruits and vegetables, meat,

fish, poultry, jewelry, drygoods, plumbing supplies, books
—everything imaginable. Most of the stands are still there
today.

But this was not a marketplace for the uninitiated.
There was a trick and an art in the intricate process of
purchasing on Maxwell Street. You had to avoid appearing
overly interested in buying. As you passed by, a merchant
would gently take you by the arm and deliver a sales talk
extolling the quality and economy of his merchandise.
Your role was to feign indifference. Gradually you would
ease up and with a deprecating tone ask coldly, "How
much?" The merchant would tell you it's a "special price
—for you only."

Actually he's losing money, he tells you. It's just a sale
he wants; it's bad luck, especially if you're his first customer, to let you go without a sale. As you hear his price,
you appear shocked and horrified at such exorbitance. "It's
highway robbery!" you exclaim and put the stuff down,
making a break to walk away. Then he comes down a little
on his price. But you won't relent. You continue the same
procedure several times, until a compromise is reached.

But not everyone came to buy, especially on Sunday,
the biggest day. People came to look, to get prices, or
merely to take a walk, to stop for a hot dog or a coke.

A good part of the Maxwell Street Market business was
illegal. Stands on the sidewalk and street were forbidden by
city ordinance, but no one ever questioned anything. Every
merchant paid his regular fee to the "market master" and
was thus protected. In addition, the market master performed, for a price, other services for the merchants. Merchants in the produce business were required by law to
provide their own scavengers to carry away their garbage,
but for a price and a few gifts in merchandise, the city
garbage collectors obliged.

Attempts to modernize the market were made several
years ago. Its face was to be lifted by an edict which re-

quired every merchant to purchase a stand that was uniform with others. Every merchant complied, but a handsome sum was charged by the forces in power. The market had its face lifted for a fleeting moment and soon reverted to its old look.

But in the old days Maxwell Street was more than a marketplace; it was a distinct social and cultural entity without parallel in the city. The patent medicine salesman, the gypsy fortune-teller, the magician, the card shark, the politician and his lesser subordinates, all contributed to the mosaic.

I remember how in those days moonshine stills were abundant. As you passed by certain houses you could smell the yeast which was used in the manufacture of alcohol. One night a still exploded, severely damaging the home of one of our neighbors. The family, which consisted of four children in addition to the parents, knocked on our door in the middle of the night asking for shelter. Inadequate as were our already cramped quarters, we admitted them to our home and shared what we had with them. This meant that most of us slept on the floor for several weeks.

I remember also when in the middle of the night we were awakened by frantic knocking at our door. Frightened, my mother inquired about the identity of these visitors in the night. "Anita, Anita, open the door, it's me, your brother Andrea." We were stunned. Andrea from Marsala! How could he be here! How did he get here? Finally my mother opened the door—and sure enough, there was Andrea, with two companions.

After we all calmed down we learned the story. My uncle and his friends were fugitives. They had gotten jobs as sailors in Italy on a freighter which delivered cargo to Texas. Then they had abandoned ship and somehow had come to Chicago and arrived at our modest abode. Well, this meant more sleeping on the floor for a few more weeks.

My uncle's companions soon went to relatives in other cities. He stayed with us and worked in a factory. After six months he decided to go to Detroit, where he lived in the home of my mother's sister. Later he went to San Francisco and became a prosperous fisherman. Before he died at the age of 55, he had the satisfaction of having become a naturalized citizen.

Frequently, we became aware of the violence, tragedy, and death that stalked the streets. One day one of our neighbors was killed in a nearby alley, suspended on a pole, and garrotted by the throat with wire. Many such events were announced by the men who paced the streets shouting the news as they tried to sell newspapers. With the advent of radio and television, those newsmen happily ceased to have a function. Their tactics had a disturbing effect on many households; they shouted the news, but so vaguely and mysteriously that no one could understand it. Since your curiosity was greatly aroused, you had no alternative but to drop everything and go out and buy the paper —for twice the usual price. Frequently the news was not so startling as the newsmen led you to believe.

Lawlessness was on the streets in those days. Young men in their newly acquired automobiles would race furiously down the streets whipping the corners, while the police frequently gave chase. This was the height of the Roaring Twenties, when youthful gangs were riding high and mighty. Most famous was the Forty two Gang, a daring, fearless lot at open warfare with the police and society. They were easily identified by their attractive white felt hats, then in vogue. The newspapers called them hoodlums, and the police pursued them relentlessly. To us younger kids they were just young men like the others— only we respected and admired them more. My sister and her friends, I recall, spoke highly of these fellows. They may have engaged in "gang shag" activities—that is, mass sexual intercourse—with girls outside the neighborbood. But they did not molest local girls; with them they were gentlemen in every sense of the word.

These young men, along with the older men in organized crime, were the heroes of our day. They had "class"
and they had "guts." Which reminds me of a story recently
told to me by a friend.

He said, "When I was a boy I broke a window at a local
settlement house and a social worker got ahold of me and
reprimanded me for my misconduct. She raised a stern and
threatening finger and said, 'Now do you want to grow up
to be a big gangster like Machine Gun Jack McGurn or
Diamond Joe and Al Capone?' In answer to this pointed
question I meekly answered, 'No'; but I really meant yes.
After all, these men were the big shots in my community—
they were successful and powerful. Hell, they were our civic
leaders—men with the greatest prestige. Naturally I wanted
to be like them. But sensing the type of response the social
worker expected, I lied and said, 'No.' "

Other sides to life in our area were bright and cheerful
and gay, for where there are human beings there will also
be song and dance and laughter. We had birthday parties
where we'd spin the bottle and play kissing games. We had
feast days, holidays, and special occasions at home when
the tables were colorfully laden with food and delicacies.
Sometimes we "snuck" into neighborhood weddings at local halls for free eats, but especially to dance with girls; here
we had a chance to satisfy that compelling urge to hold our
neighborhood girls close.

On warm summer evenings fire hydrants were opened
to refresh the air and wash off the children's sweltering
bodies, while older men and women sat outside their
houses watching and telling tales of old. Men would play
bocci and *amorra* and drink the wine which one *compare* or
paesani or neighbor had brought out.

Speaking of wine reminds me that in those days most
families made their own wine and did much of their own
canning, especially of tomatoes. For the wine, the men
would go to the railroad yards where the grapes were

brought in and order their load; others would buy the grapes from peddlers who came into the neighborhood. When a load of grapes was sold—100 to 200 boxes, each weighing approximately 40 pounds—the kids would all flock to the scene for the pleasure of helping to carry the boxes into the basement wine cellar. The reward was eating all the grapes you could, plus getting a big bunch to take home.

Also colorful and exciting were the religious processions, usually preceding the opening of a street carnival sponsored by one of the many fraternal societies. Led by a band, men would carry a statue of the patron saint. Kids would follow the band and the statue through the streets, and occasionally pious men and women would signal that they wished to make an offering. The offering consisted of paper money which was pinned on the society's banner. At the end of the procession the banner was fully bedecked with hundreds of dollars.

All these and many more scenes of life and love were as much a part of the life of the neighborhood as was its gloom, tragedy, and death.

Chapter 2

INFERIORITY AND ENTHUSIASM

BRIDGING THE GAP

Although I was sensitive to the general social world I was thrust into when I was six years old, I became even more aware of it as I grew up in the midst of poverty, a fatherless home, and great uncertainty about the future. My driving ambition was to finish grammar school and go to work. I remained in school under compulsion, daydreaming much of the time, wondering and hoping for a better future. Among other reasons, I detested school because I had to wear patched short trousers long after I was ready for long pants. Without the aid of a father in our home, my prospects seemed hopeless and bewildering, and my feelings of inferiority and inadequacy worsened.

It was because of these feelings that one summer day in 1928 I reacted so quickly to Henry A. Meyer. Here was a man who constructively influenced my life from the moment I met him. He was a theology student who was working part time as a playground director and boys' worker for the local Italian Methodist Church. He and his wife seemed to be so kind and friendly that I reacted with all the boundless enthusiasm and thirst that a growing boy in a deprived situation is capable of showing. When Mr. Meyer organized a scout troop, I quit the troop I belonged to and joined his. He encouraged me by giving me responsibilities he thought I could carry out.

He was also the first person to introduce me to literature. The few books I had read at this time were the Tom Swift and Rover Boy series. When I graduated from grammar school, Mr. Meyer and his wife gave me a copy of *The Three Musketeers* by Alexander Dumas, the first book I ever received as a gift. I enjoyed this book, but it was more difficult to read than the others. I then read *Tom Sawyer* and became an avid reader and admirer of Mark Twain. I started collecting his books and others, which soon led to my lifelong hobby. To this day, I can hardly pass a bookstore without going in, and if it's a second-hand bookstore I will invariably go in and browse around. Before long I was bringing home too many books to please my mother. Her concern was twofold. First, there wasn't enough room in our small four-room flat to build a library. Secondly, how in the world could I ever read all those books? Besides, I could not become a professor, so why bother with too many books. After a while she seemed to say, "Enough is enough!"

But her objections were to no avail. I continued to bring books into the house without her knowing it, hiding them wherever I could. Later, she mellowed. At times, with a warm glow on her face, she would say, "Who knows, maybe you will be a professor or a lawyer. After all, when you were born they didn't raise the flag on your father's ship for nothing."

A crowning achievement was when Mr. Meyer selected me to give a three-minute talk on the radio for the boy scout finance drive. My elation could not have been greater, though at the same time I felt miserably inadequate to the task. I couldn't understand why he selected me when there were other boys who were much better equipped. When I asked him, he cordially replied, "George and Leonard are not dependable. They might not show up, but I know you won't let us down." Obviously I did not, and the experience was terrifically gratifying when a picture of me with several prominent men appeared in the newspaper.

I have reflected on this experience ever since and, of course, the whole idea is very simple. This man felt that he could depend on me; he knew I was loyal. I have used this simple rule as a guiding principle. If one is conscientious, dependable, and loyal in his work or with his friends, he can easily compensate for some of his shortcomings.

My relationship with Henry A. Meyer, which lasted for many years after he moved out of the neighborhood, also gave me my first introduction to youth welfare work and suggested how the church can have a constructive impact if it reaches out in the community. Although not a large or significant institution in the Italian community, the Italian Methodist Church sponsored a neighborhood center and playground adjoining its church at Polk and Carpenter streets. I met Henry Meyer here. I attended the neighborhood center and was introduced to books, crafts, and American food. Actually the people were so friendly and congenial that it's a wonder I didn't join the Methodist church.

The influences of custom and tradition were clearly at work here. While not all Italians are great churchgoers, 99 percent will say they are Catholics. And even those who attend infrequently, if at all, will baptize their children in the Church, have them make their first Communion and Confirmation, and get married and buried in the Church. While my parents were in that category of poor churchgoers, they adhered to all the above practices, and instilled in me as a child was the feeling that to become a Protestant was forbidden and alien. Even to enter a Protestant church was sinful and would bring bad luck! Thus, although I participated in the social activities at the storefront center sponsored by the Methodist church, I never attended the services. Only once, as I recall, enticed by a girl, did I even dare open the church door for a furtive glance, and after that I quickly ran away.

Henry Meyer was the first person who helped give me a glimpse outside the neighborhood and prepare me for later adventures. The new vistas he opened up to me were considerably in contrast to certain aspects of life in my neighborhood, with its delinquency, crime, and violence, so rampant in the 1920s and early 1930s. This man started to give me the feeling that perhaps, after all, I too might be regarded as a valued member of society.

This has since made me realize what is involved in the task of helping troubled persons—whether they be emotionally disturbed, insecure, or delinquent—overcome some of their difficulties. Because this experience had a beneficial effect on my life, it made me realize that the fundamental problem of aiding the delinquent or the mentally ill or any person who is out of tune with his environment is to find a person or a group that will receive and welcome the individual and in a friendly, helpful, understanding spirit give that person the feeling he is liked, wanted, and respected. If that person is dealt with in this manner and in addition furnished constructive guidance—new and better incentives, ideals, and opportunities—his rehabilitation would seem to be assured.

The conditioning effect of poverty and slum life are not easily erased, however, and the early feelings of inferiority kept recurring, particularly after Mr. Meyer moved out of the city. But with the strong crutches he had provided, I was able to keep struggling until opportunities became available.

In June 1928, when not yet 15 years of age, I graduated from the Andrew Jackson Elementary School. I was determined to find a job. There were dozens of factories within walking distance of my neighborhood, but for some reason I decided to call on several printing companies. In some vague way I thought that perhaps working in a print shop would lead to higher things. After all, hadn't Ben Franklin gotten his start in this humble way! I also had another strategy: I would call on several print shops regularly. Week after week the shop foreman would inform me that there were no jobs. But I kept on calling. Finally, one man with a serious expression called me aside and said, "Look, lad, I appreciate your determination, and that's a good quality. Believe me, if I had a job you would get it."

That man sounded sincere, and although I was discouraged I did not feel completely rebuffed. There would come the day. That happy day arrived shortly after, when Mr. Meyer took me to an employment agency downtown. I had to lie about my age, saying I was 17, and I was offered a job in the Loop—as an office boy at $12 a week with the Sardeson-Hoveland Company, which operated a chain of women's apparel stores in small towns, mostly in the Midwest.

My mother gave credit to Santo Antonio Di Padua for my luck in getting this job. She had made a pledge to Saint Anthony that if I was fortunate in finding a job she would send $5 as an offering to our church in Marsala. She, of course, kept the promise, and we received a large portrait as an inducement to send more favors, especially when looking for lost articles; for Saint Anthony is the patron saint who is supposed to guide finders seeking lost objects or lost causes.

Because I had nothing to anchor to in my own community as a means of moving up in the world, I vaguely sensed that somehow I must try to fit myself into the outside world. That objective, as we shall see, did not materialize.

I had no further interest in going to school. I had been just an average pupil, with no attraction whatsoever to intellectual pursuits. I wanted to work with my hands. But the office job had much influence on my later occupations. The neat, clean, businesslike atmosphere of the office and the contacts with many people in the office building were in great contrast to the spirit of poverty of my home and the drab environment of my neighborhood. This sudden change to a different social world had a profound effect upon my attitudes and outlook in the world. Here all about me were people I regarded as successful. They had good incomes, compared with mine; a number of them had incomes that would assure them a place in the social register. I lived amidst wealth, opulence, and big business during the day but had to retreat to a hovel, comparatively speaking, at the end of the day.

At the office I sat at a desk befitting any big executive, but at home I sat at a broken-down kitchen table. The gulf between the two worlds was staggering. Gradually I decided to do something about it. How was I, a meagerly equipped boy, going to compete in such a world? My education and my social experiences were inadequate for participation in this new social setting.

At first I wanted to run away from all this. It was impossible, I thought, for me to participate in this new world. I was self-conscious of my sparse and clumsy vocabulary, which included "dees and dose," "dis and dat," and the other typical jargon of the streets. It took me a long time to learn to pronounce the "th" sounds. I was nervous when speaking in the presence of the self-composed, complacent office manager, and always uneasy in the presence of the officers of the firm. But I just had to stick to this job, despite the uncomfortable and sickening feelings which for many months assailed me.

I went to night school to learn to manipulate the type-writer which was beside me at the office all day. Encouraged also by a few boys from my neighborhood who went to night high school, I proceeded to take other courses so that after six years, together with special home study courses, I completed my high school education.

After a few years of office work, plus the confidence which schooling was developing, I came to feel more at ease. I especially noticed this feeling when the boss's son came to work with us for a few weeks during vacation time. To my delight I noticed that he was green in some respects. I had to teach him some of the office routines. I noticed that he was in strange territory when he tried to operate some of the simple office machines—stamping, mimeograph, and addressograph machines. He was a nice chap, and I rather liked him. We would go to lunch together and talk of some of the adventure stories we had read. But the boss's son stopped coming around after a few weeks, and I had an uncanny idea about the reason. The boss didn't want his son, who lived in a $50,000 home, associating too inti-mately with the lowly office boy who lived in a low income area.

This was further evidence that if I wished to find a place for myself—after all, I couldn't continue being an office boy at $18 a week for all my life—I couldn't expect any open sesame opportunities such as the boss's son would inevitably fall into. I had to struggle and fight and work if I wished to assure myself some of the economic and social opportunities which everyone strives for.

I was always conscious of the great disparity between the various social situations I moved in. While at work I was always—and I mean always—aware of the fact that people I worked with all had superior economic resources; better clothes, better homes, and better opportunities for recre-ation and education. The mere thought of this difference would make me feel miserable.

As the all-around office boy, I also performed a number of personal favors for the office executives, including delivering packages to their homes. I would always come away emotionally upset. These homes represented another world, distant and unattainable. And as I would leave, the pictures of these nice steam-heated houses with beautiful carpets, drapes, and elegant furniture kept swimming in my mind. I would feel bitter and frustrated.

However, I had many other companions in my own neighborhood, and since our homes and parents' backgrounds were similar we were at ease with each other. My friends at this older adolescent period were of two types: the corner boys and the college boys. Although I maintained contacts with corner boys on an individual basis (several went to jail), I began to develop much closer ties with the boys who were aspiring toward higher education.

But I kept meeting many of the corner boys at dance halls and later in correctional institutions. I remember one occasion a few years later when I went with a criminology class on a field trip to the Cook County Jail. As we were shown around by one of the guards, I saw one of the inmates, an old friend, doing maintenance work. I was so surprised to encounter him in this way that I spontaneously went up to him, shook hands, and exchanged courtesies. Instantly the guards came up to us and searched both of us. This scene, of course, elicited varied interesting responses from my professor and classmates.

One of the college boys was Vito Lucatorto, who was in medical school and today is a physician. We visited at each other's homes, studied together, went to movies and to the big ballrooms, which were flourishing in that era of the big bands, for dancing. Few people had cars, and hence we always traveled by streetcar or bus. Through Vito, one day I met Peter Scalise at a local center when Alonzo Stagg, the famous football coach, was speaking. From that moment on, Pete and I became truly close friends and spent much time together studying and talking for endless hours about many personal and social concerns. We were quite idealistic, and gradually we both became very actively involved in the community organization which I discuss in this book.

Joining this intimate group a few years later was Joseph Giunta, an earthy, vigorous person who came up the hard way; he was truly our finest example of an indigenous leader. He worked actively in our many civic and community projects and was later employed, as I was, with the state as a community worker on the Near West Side. Today he has responsibility for a statewide program, as assistant director of the Illinois Commission on Delinquency Prevention.

This intimate friendship of four close friends—Doc, Pete, Joe, and myself—has continued uninterrupted for over 40 years, and we are actually closer in many ways than we are with relatives. To this day, our children refer to us and our spouses as "uncle" or "aunt." In addition, we are also *compare* and *commare,* since we have served back and forth as best men at each other's weddings or as godparents' for our children at their baptisms or confirmations.

Another friend who had an impact on me was Seymour Nash, introduced to me by Pete Scalise. Seymour was a Russian Jew who lived just west of our neighborhood and attended Crane Junior College with Pete. His parents were Orthodox Jews and very poor. One son was a truck driver, and a daughter later had a career in the health field. But Seymour! I thought he was the smartest guy that ever lived! Soon after I had met him he was studying at the University of Chicago, and I was merely going to evening high school at Crane. Occasionally on Saturday afternoon after working at Sardeson and Hoveland, we used to go to the downtown library to study or visit the Art Institute. He knew poetry, literature, art, and music and could converse intelligently for hours. I remember once we went to the Rockefeller

Chapel at the University of Chicago to hear Jane Addams give a lecture and then attended a social function in one of the university halls. This was a different kind of crowd than I had been used to, and it was my first introduction to the world of liberals and others who in these Depression days were considered left-wing and radical.

Another interesting activity which Seymour introduced me to on Saturday afternoon was to be an usher at the Auditorium Theater. No pay, but after everyone was seated you saw the plays. I vividly remember seeing the musical *Of Thee I Sing* and other plays which I enjoyed. One play, however, which I thought a little odd, was written by Gertrude Stein. After we came out of the theater I remember we kept repeating, "Pigeons on the grass, alas, alas!" or "A rose is a rose is a rose."

Seymour had hopes of becoming a professor, but upon completing his undergraduate degree he got married and hence had to work. He taught education courses for a few years and later received a master's degree and became a social worker. But his career was shortlived. He died of cancer in his early thirties.

Being in college at age 21 was no more comforting or assuring than when I was in grammar school. What was I to become? Who would help me? My family was living on a poverty level. I had no rich uncle to subsidize me. My friends were also struggling. My meaningful contacts and relationships were all limited to people in my own community, and these did not include the more successful businessmen or politicians. My family was a simple, small, humble unit with not even one vote in it to entice the local precinct captain to furnish useful contacts. (My mother did not become naturalized until many years later.) In other words, the outside world with its opportunities and resources was inaccessible to me.

This was especially disturbing during the Depression, when for six months I was unemployed and aimlessly paced the streets in search of a job. I would walk through the downtown streets and see wealth all around, men with positions, influence, and power. How did these people do it? What does it take? I searched for answers in my then naïve way, but always ended up against a stone wall.

I would walk through the Near West Side, an area referred to by sociologists of the period in terms of "physical deterioration, bad housing, overcrowding, poverty, crime and delinquency, low rents, low family income, a disproportionate percentage of families on relief or dependent on public agencies for support, and the highest incidence of social problems."

To the east of the area I would see the industrial district; railroad terminals and large garages for trucks and buses for Loop department stores and other businesses. To the north, I would walk through a rooming-house area that stretched for miles along and around Madison Street. Here were people who had come to Chicago to find better jobs, but even those who eventually succeeded had had to stay in this gloomy, terrifying environment for a time. Others living there were only waiting to die and in the meantime escaped their misery by drinking cheap whiskey or even wood alcohol. Found dead from such causes, they were hurried to the county morgue and buried in Potter's Field or sent to a nearby medical school for the students to study their cadavers.

This was the area of taverns, honky-tonks, houses of prostitution, taxi-dance halls, burlesque shows, shooting galleries, greasy spoon eating joints, poolrooms, and other attractions. It was here that boys from our neighborhood would practice jackrolling drunks, and boys 15 or 16 years old came here to look for their first rendezvous with the opposite sex, a necessary condition for being a "man." This is where I had labored as a shoeshine boy. Only now things were different; there were more homeless men than before, more vagrants milling around on corners where

soap-box orators, radicals, and Communists were herald-
ing the new order. I listened to some of these speakers and
wondered.

Life seemed bleak and harsh, with no bright future on
the horizon. All these impressions and scenes created a
sense of frustration, helplessness, and conflict. Had I continued having such experiences for a longer period than six
months, I don't know what I might have done. Several of
my street-corner buddies who were having similar experiences turned to crime and spent many years in prison. But
for the grace of God, I too might have followed the same
path. The saving factor was the Chicago Area Project.

BEGINNING A NEW ADVENTURE

When a group of us neighborhood high school boys first
heard about the Chicago Area Project in 1933, we responded enthusiastically. Our first introduction to it was
one Sunday afternoon when Clifford Shaw spoke to our
group at a meeting at Hull House. He first spoke about the
problem of delinquency, presenting some of his findings
from *Delinquency Areas.* He indicated that the earlier immigrant groups in the city had high rates of delinquency
which tended to go down as these groups improved their
social and economic position. He stated that although the
rates of delinquency and crime were high among Italians,
in time they too would decrease.

His views were refreshing, since we Italians were then
being stigmatized by the public and the press. For some
time we had been hoping that we could do something to
improve the reputation of our area. We learned what we
could do through the Chicago Area Project. High school
boys that we were, we were too young to assume responsibility for such a great task, although we were in it from the

beginning and later took over the leadership when the first
community council became too fragmented to be effective.

The potentials for leadership in our community were
present in our people, but they were dormant until stimulated and encouraged by Clifford R. Shaw and his associates. These people did not come to us in the spirit of
philanthropy; they did not believe in handouts or lady
bountiful approaches. They felt that people of our community could get together to discuss and develop a program
for dealing with our problems that would employ our own
initiative in an enterprise of our own, while they played the
role of catalyst.

For many years, agencies from outside our community
had come to do uplift work—and yes, to foster leadership
in the community, but only in a very limited way, from the
top down. Either they regarded us as inferior to the task or
they felt that a retinue of trained workers was the only
qualified group.

The first Area Project worker on the Near West Side
was Mark Alderman. He stayed in close contact with us
boys and instilled in us the spirit and principles of the
Chicago Area Project. He encouraged us to form a permanent club in order to make a stronger bond among us. His
oft-repeated remark, "Tall oaks from little acorns grow,"
was an inspiring slogan. Eventually the acorn took root,
and it slowly developed into a sturdy oak, as Alderman had
hoped it would.

We followed his suggestion and organized the Guiding
Brothers, a teenage club with the loftiest set of principles
imaginable. We were solemnly serious! We felt the responsibility heavily on our shoulders. We oozed inspiration and
enthusiasm and foresaw the day when we would be outstanding civic leaders and our community would be put on
the map. We would show the world what we could do! We
would buckle down and show them that the Italians were
not all street cleaners, factory hands, unskilled laborers,

illiterates, and such. We would show them that we could become valuable leaders in our community and make a constructive contribution to our city.

We met almost every week, discussing our problems and making plans for the future. We talked to the young men and urged them to join us. Occasionally we sponsored picnics and outings, serving a social purpose in addition to formulating our idealistic goals. In our meetings we learned from guest speakers about the writings of Guiseppe Mazzini and the deeds of Guiseppe Garibaldi, two of the foremost militant leaders in the unification movement of Italy in the nineteenth century. We were inspired by the humanistic philosophy of Mazzini the intellectual, and by the organizing abilities and action strategies of Garibaldi the soldier. The qualities of these leaders and Shaw's charisma helped to infuse us with a sense of mission: to improve our community, prevent delinquency, and enhance the status of our ethnic group.

Such was our enthusiasm as the first Area Project worker came into our midst. As Mr. Alderman made contacts with the more prominent business and professional men of our area, we observed the steps he took to establish our first community council. Mr. Alderman found ready interest in our community for this idea, and a good number of people rallied to the cause. He met them individually and in groups and attended their social functions. With his broad grin and expansive personality, he made friends quickly. Before long he was invited to the homes of our people for spaghetti and ravioli dinners. He accepted and drank a tumbler of wine like a man. He joined in the card games and the bocci games of the older men, and he kept up with the lingo of the boys on the street. No highbrow, he was an easygoing guy who made himself at home everywhere. After several months, about 50 men representing our district banded together and organized the West Side Community Council.

The Area Project furnished Mr. Alderman's services as a consultant to the council and also hired one of our young men, Guy De Filippis a college graduate, to help direct the program. In addition, the Area Project made available several thousand dollars in the beginning and each year thereafter to finance the council's program.

At first the council met in homes of members and in the local institutions. But soon it had to find a home, a place where it could meet, transact its business, and carry on some of its activities. An abandoned brick building formerly used as a stable on Vernon Park Place near Racine Avenue was purchased at a reasonable price with funds raised by the council and by the Area Project. The building was shortly after renovated and an additional structure added by the Public Works Administration.

The renovation of the building to serve as a community center required over two years. Meanwhile the council met in a stove-heated room and carried on social and recreational activities in the community. Our Lady of Pompeii Church, located nearby, offered the use of its large basement for clubrooms and recreational activities. The workers were furnished by a state project known as the Children's Leisure Time Service, another agency that sought to alleviate the unemployment situation in the 1930s. Approximately 15 young men from the neighborhood, including myself and other members of our Guiding Brothers' Club, secured employment on this project, and an equal number of men and some women from other areas were assigned to work in connection with this project.

I knew little of what was going to happen in 1934 when, as a disillusioned young man of 21, I was unemployed and had no means of contributing to the support of my family. Interested in it or not, my first consideration was survival. When I was offered a job as a recreational leader on the streets by the Chicago Area Project and our local community council, I was dubious and uncertain. I asked myself, "What kind of racket is this? Am I interested in recreation, in social work? Am I trained and equipped?" That feeling of inferiority that had been ingrained in me as a product of a "river ward," as people from uptown referred to our community, kept recurring as I was about to set out on this new adventure. That summer of 1934, I reported to work.

In the early days of work-relief programs, the emphasis was first on putting people on the payroll and only then finding work for them. Needed or not, the council found itself before long with 30 to 40 workers—students, former clerks, laborers, and others who had never held jobs, though of employable age.

Mr. Alderman knew of my interest in my community because as a member of the Guiding Brothers I had talked with him about it. Above all I needed a job, so he arranged to have me assigned as a recreation leader to work with the boys' gangs in my neighborhood. A few other members of our group also worked in this project. Together we started to get our first experience in the field of community organizing.

Part II

THE ORGANIZATION
AND THE NEIGHBORHOOD

We cannot change habit directly: that notion is magic. But we can change it indirectly by modifying conditions, by an intelligent selecting and weighing of the objects which engage attention and which influence the fulfillment of desires.

John Dewey

You have to remember that concepts which are accepted today were considered wildly radical then—for instance, the idea that local people have the intelligence and the ingenuity to work out their own problems.

Saul Alinsky

Chapter 3

GETTING ORGANIZED

FROM COUNCIL TO COMMITTEE

The stable where the council first met still smelled like a stable and was to require several years before it became a boys' club and community center. Until it was ready, we worked in the neighborhood, literally on the sidewalks, streets, empty lots, basements, homes, and corner hangouts. We worked with small natural groups or gangs in their own habitats. Later these informal play groups were organized into teams and clubs and entered into community-wide tournaments.

In launching this program, the block system was adopted. Each worker was assigned to two or three blocks to enlist the interest and participation of neighborhood adults and function as a group leader for the gangs in the neighborhood. In the very beginning, a bat and ball constituted our only equipment. But we used other resources in the informal play situations of the children: street games, peg and stick, handicraft with a knife, club meetings in corner hangouts, and trips to museums and forest preserves—these were some of our activities for about a year.

Each member of our staff worked with about three small gangs; this made it possible for us to have rather extensive coverage of the boys' gangs in the whole community. We made special efforts to work with those gangs that were labeled delinquent and that were not welcome at other community centers in the district. It was a cardinal principle with us at the outset to make special efforts to reach delinquent children in our area, to receive and welcome them, and to make every effort to incorporate them into our activities and general program. Forty years later this would still be our paramount objective. Meanwhile, the council broadened its membership, publicized its goals, and did much to arouse community interest in local problems, particularly through its *Community News,* on which I served as a feature writer.

This council established the beginnings of our self-help community enterprise. After functioning from 1934 to 1938, it decided to relinquish responsibility for the management of the community center, since funds from outside the community were needed to operate the large plant. Since ours was a predominantly Catholic community, the council and the Area Project decided it would be best to invite Bishop Sheil, founder and director of the Catholic Youth Organization, to assume the responsibility for the operation of the community center. Bishop Sheil accepted this responsibility and agreed with the council's provisions that the CYO organize a board of directors of community residents to assist in the management of the center. This they did, and the CYO and the committee worked together on various projects. This continued until the late 1950s, when the building housing the center was purchased by the Department of Urban Renewal and demolished to make way for new housing.

Shortly after the responsibility for operating the community center was given to the CYO, members of our Guiding Brothers felt that our enterprise could stand a shot in the arm. The members of the council also welcomed new blood, and we were encouraged by them and by Area Project representatives to band together. When a nucleus of Guiding Brothers got together and talked things over at informal gatherings at our homes and at the center, we soon realized we could enlist many other young men and that we would be free to formulate our own program and make our own plans.

In the fall of 1938 we thus reorganized the council and decided to call ourselves the West Side Community Committee. In March 1939 we became incorporated as a not-for-profit organization. It was apparent to us, however, that for our group to gain strength and carry on the work it needed funds to get started and to establish a headquarters of its own. Since our relationships with Shaw and his associates of the Area Project continued, we naturally depended on them for support. To our surprise we learned that the Area Project was willing to make available $1,700 for our first year's budget, provide my services as the business manager and program director, and assist us in making available other resources.

There were a number of skeptical members in our group who were suspicious of any agency's motives. They were reluctant to believe that any organization would contribute a large amount of money on such liberal terms, and they kept repeating, "There must be some catch to this offer. It's not possible for anyone to be so trusting and generous." It was only after much debate that the group voted to accept the Area Project offer. The skeptics later said this was the best thing they ever voted for.

Our group of approximately 50 young men was typical of the community. A number were on relief or employed on relief projects, others were clerks or businessmen, and a few were professional people. The unifying bond of our group was simply that we were all young men, ranging in age from 21 to 35, with the average age being about 25. We were all products of our community and of the depression-ridden and proletariat '30's. We all had the same basic motivations: to find a good job, to have security, and to succeed in life.

Some of us sensed the extreme difficulty and at times the futility of obtaining better social and economic opportunities. I remember meeting two young men who were bitter and hard. When I asked about their frame of mind, they first cursed and blasphemed the whole universe. For the moment these young men seemed to have lost all hope. What terrible thing had happened to them? Having gone for a job where they knew there were openings, they had been given the cold shoulder with the usual "we'll let you know." Outside they met a friend who sympathetically chuckled that they'd better forget all about it. He explained that the manager was not hiring Italians from that area because of its "hoodlum background."

Here were two small, easygoing chaps who had not been engaged in crime but who were suspected of being criminals. "Goddamn it, if people think we're hoodlums, well then we ought to be," they said.

Some friends of mine from Taylor Street, a well-known thoroughfare which connotes "Little Italy," moved out of the area into a community occupied predominantly by native Americans. This young couple hadn't lived there a week before rumors and gossip about them began to bounce around to this effect: "Be careful about those Italians, especially those from Taylor and Halsted." A few months later, an elderly couple who lived in the building next door was robbed of $9,000 in cash. The young Italian couple was immediately suspected. The first house the police pounded on was theirs. A group of stern and determined policemen was about to prance in when the young wife asserted herself and called them down for their militant attitude. They calmed down and questioned her and got their information, then left.

This young man was a conscientious, law-abiding citizen, a skilled workman with a quiet, devoted love for his family. Hurt, he told us, "Yes, we Italians from the Near West Side sure got a bad reputation, but nobody is going to push me around like those cops tried to."

This is not to single out the police; they were no more or less kindly disposed toward our people than the wider society was. But over the years they operated in our community with an aggressive, "crack down and push them around" policy—that is, until later, when our people assumed a more commanding position. But even after that happened, many of our younger men remembered the old approach and were still subjected to it in milder forms.

Some chaps from a club in our area related the following story to illustrate how "the cops still pick on us." A young man, whom they stressed was absolutely above reproach as regards his law-abiding conduct—a steadily employed worker, frugal, and serious-minded—was stopped as he was driving his newly purchased car. The police suspected him of something and directed him to drive to the station for questioning. As they were driving there, a bunch of fellows from the corner spotted him and guessed the situation. They whistled for a political leader who happened to be nearby, and he stopped the police. When the police were given the chap's background, they left him alone in a hurry.

The ravages of poverty, poor schooling, delinquency habits, inadequate health care, and limited social relationships—all these were indelibly imprinted on our personalities, as was the doubt, despair, confusion, and fear in the United States during those days. What was the alternative? Succumb to our misery? Rely on relief or WPA? Have the long arm of centralized government solve our problems?

Surely government help was desirable and needed, but we needed something more fundamental. We needed a group, an enterprise in which we could come together, pool our talents and resources, and take the lead in solving our own problems.

If it was true that our community was famous for its traditions of delinquency, well then, why not deliberately set out, slowly to be sure, to develop a tradition of constructive leadership, of social and civic advancement? We would create a prideful tradition.

We were not thinking in terms of a limited clientele, a number of specific groupwork activities with a clear-cut physical plant. We always thought about the welfare of the whole community and regarded the constellation of agencies and institutions as part of a whole community structure. We were vitally concerned with the problems of our local schools, with the relation of the settlements, community centers, and public parks to our people, and with the vital role of our religious and political institutions.

WELFARE AGENCIES: ALIEN AND AUTONOMOUS

Early in our work we were aware of the artificial distinctions in the welfare field and the lack of cooperation among agencies that had been operating on the Near West Side for well over half a century. As the people and indigenous leaders, we felt that one of the fundamental changes we ought to help bring about was to overcome the isolation, social distance, and impersonal relationships between the people and their institutions and even between the agencies and the local institutions.

Before setting up an office or central headquarters where we could transact our affairs, we decided to get further aquainted with the work of the local agencies and institutions. We held our meetings in some of the local

agencies for several months. This experience gave some of
the men their first opportunity to see the inside of a social
agency.

The idea underlying our organization was a radical
departure from traditional agency work. In going to some
of these local institutions we said, "We, the young men of
the community, would like to come in here and meet you
and your staff to discuss the problems of our children and
of the community. We would like to know what your institution is attempting to do in this regard; then we would like
to suggest how we might cooperate with you in dealing with
these problems."

To our knowledge, this was the first time in the history
of welfare work on the Near West Side of Chicago that any
group so boldly set forth to request the participation of the
area's residents in the management of such enterprises.
Some agencies responded warmly to the proposal, while
others were lukewarm and indifferent; but in general we
developed a pretty good working relationship with them
and, over the years, we believe we succeeded, at least par-
tially, in overcoming the alienations between our community and local institutions.

A distinction may here be noted in the relation of these
institutions to our community. We may categorize institutions as indigenous or superimposed. The indigenous institutions—the church, the social and athletic clubs, the
fraternal organizations, the gangs, the local political organizations—those embody the sentiments, the values, and
the ideals of the people. Growing out of the basic needs of
the people themselves, they emerge spontaneously, and
they are under their leadership. The practices of these institutions are thus not alien to the people, because they
represent values and ways of behaving which are rooted in
the culture and traditions of the groups.

On the other hand, superimposed institutions—the
settlement, community center, or social agencies generally

—do not arise spontaneously or in response to the will of the people. They are created and financed by persons from outside the community. For the most part, the residents of the community in which these superimposed institutions operate do not participate significantly in giving leadership to the work initiated by the agency, nor do they assume any responsibility for the financing or management of the institution. The hired hands of these agencies are in no way responsible to the people, but to the boards of trustees who have the authority and control. A professional worker some time ago told me, "I couldn't discharge my professional skills if the authority for my work were vested in the residents of this community because I would disagree with them about what should be done to deal with the problems." Of course, this worker had no reluctance in obeying the authority of his board of trustees.

The structure of these superimposed institutions or agencies is such that by their very nature they are isolated from the community. This type of institution often becomes a little world of its own, detached and removed from the social milieu of the neighborhood. As far as the people of our community are concerned, the boards of trustees of these agencies represent a closed group. A resident of our community has never participated as a member of the board of any of these agencies. The boards are composed almost entirely of upper-class or middle-class persons who have no dealings, except in a few formal situations, with the people of the community.

That the people may have unfavorable opinions regarding some of these institutions is often shocking news to most trustees. For example, a few years ago, a trustee of one of our local agencies was chagrined to learn that his name carried no weight in a political campaign despite the fact that his ancestors and he himself had for many years contributed heavily to social-work programs in our community.

Our work, as well as the Chicago Area Project as a whole, was viewed by many social workers as an "anti-private agency" and therefore as a threat to the established social welfare system. These and other objections to the Area Project were voiced by many social workers in the early decades. Its workers were called "undercover" agents and "untrained," and the people involved in the community committees were held to be of questionable character.

One social worker, Hasseltine Byrd Taylor, regarded the Area Project as an attempt to "fight the Devil with fire"; its use of natural leaders "is questionable and fraught with danger to the community," she said. "To expect good results from the use of such means is to expect the impossible."

Miss Taylor also disagreed with Shaw's conception of delinquency. She alleged that the Area Project viewed the problem of delinquency solely on the basis of "material and social dimensions" and ignored the "inner conflicts contributing to anti-social behavior." This social worker concluded "the activities of the Area Project to be socially dangerous."[39]

In still another document, Miss Taylor stated in a "strictly confidential investigation" of the Area Project:

> Shaw is of Irish ancestry, of a section of Ireland that has suffered domination for decades. He has acquired the purpose in life, as a result, to help the oppressed. According to one who knows him well, he really wants to help those who are poor and who live in the "blighted areas" of the city. His method is any method that will work. Consequently, he discovers the "influential" people and uses them, no matter their personal or moral standards. Ward politicians, tavern-keepers, and gamblers serve his purpose along with priests, industrialists, and capitalists. This is why Christian people have difficulty in understanding him.[40]

Later, when Miss Taylor called a series of meetings of social workers to discuss this new threat to social welfare and presumably to formulate action to deal with it, I attended one of the first sessions as a guest. Nothing significant happened, and after a lot of empty talk the meeting adjourned.

At another meeting, apparently the really big shots in the field were called in, and Shaw was given an opportunity to make a statement. As I later heard, he started out by responding to the charge that "his method is any method that will work" by saying that this was the best compliment he ever received. Jane Addams, founder and long-time leader of Hull House, commented that if the social settlement achieved its goal of Americanizing the immigrant, Shaw's idea and methods of operation should be the logical next step for the social agencies. Mayor Edward J. Kelly commented that it made sense to him to do social work by using Shaw's methods.

Rather than being a hindrance, these criticisms and accusations actually inspired everyone in our enterprise, giving us the weapons for a good fight. It was an exciting challenge, and we met it head on. From Shaw and his research colleagues down to the worker in the street, we constantly refuted these criticisms, which were either distortions or showed a complete misunderstanding of the nature of life in disadvantaged communities.

WORKING WITH LOCAL INSTITUTIONS

Because of the important role the Catholic church played in our community, it was apparent to us that we could not develop a significant community organization to deal with social problems without involving it. The Church was one of the most stable and unifying forces in the life of our people.

It seemed incredible to us that the social agencies in our area, a predominantly Catholic community, made few or no attempts to develop a close working relationship with the churches. There may have been some contacts between the area's secular and religious institutions, but certainly there was no evidence that both worked jointly on any type of welfare program. Apparently each institution felt that it had its own field or work and that the best policy was to operate there.

From the very beginning we worked closely with our parish priests, calling on them for help and counsel in planning and promoting various phases of our work. Since Rev. Remigio Pigato, pastor of Our Lady of Pompeii Church, responded enthusiastically to this invitation to work with us, we elected him our comptroller, which meant he had to countersign every check issued by our organization. Our members and the neighborhood leaders were in frequent contact with him.

We worked closely with our church and its leaders in dealing with delinquents, in operating neighborhood centers for our children, and in developing a summer camp and picnic grove. Details of this work will be given in the following chapters.

From the beginning, we also worked closely with our local public park director and staff. At first we held regular meetings at Sheridan Park. Here we were fortunate in having the attentive ear and genuine interest of William F. Steinhaus, a park director who understood our philosophy and who was eager to work with us.

Here was a public institution which was operated, for the most part, by rules, regulations, and edicts from the downtown office. From an administrative standpoint this was probably justified, but we were interested in making this a people's park, a neighborhood institution in which the people had the opportunity to voice their opinions and assist in its direction. The park director was friendly to this, so we worked together harmoniously.

The park director asked for our assistance in doing

something about the problem of broken windows. Our children were prone to use the park windows as targets for their excess energy. The windows were enticing to the boys who rambled along the park property, especially at night or on weekends when the park staff was not there. Most of the children who broke the windows also attended classes at the park. But apparently this participation in itself was not enough to give them a significant role in the institution.

We suggested that some of these troublesome boys, as well as other boys who exhibited constructive leadership, be hired to perform part-time tasks at the park. Our committee provided a small fund, and some of these boys were put to work. Interestingly, a few of the champion window-breakers were given a dollar a week to polish the windows. Others polished door knobs. Others were attendants in the shower room. Others picked up broken pieces of glass from the park field. And others did clerical work. Some of these boys were made group leaders in charge of small play groups under the supervision of the athletic instructors or members of our recreation committee.

The people took over some of the activities at the park. We enhanced the amount and quality of the activities in many ways. We sponsored a large number of athletic tournaments and enlisted the participation of the neighborhood clubs and teams in community-wide activities. We purchased medals and trophies and displayed them in local stores so that everyone could see them. We presented the awards to the champions in school assemblies or in special public ceremonies at the park.

We also financed other educational activities at the park. We invited local groups to make more extensive use of park facilities. We capitalized on the artistic ability of an older boy and got him to organize a class in cartooning. We purchased materials for craft and sewing classes and made available other funds for special occasions as the need arose.

By making available some funds for program expenses to the park, our committee assisted in expanding the work of that institution. The Chicago Park District did not provide the local parks with funds for program expenses; consequently, parks in low-income areas like ours could operate only a rather standardized program within the confines of the park facilities. By manifesting our interest and contributing our leadership and a small amount of money, we were able over a period of years to make our park a more meaningful institution, better equipped to meet the needs of our children, young people, and adults. Forty years ago, Sheridan Park was considered a liability by the officials of the park district. In later years they regarded this park as one of the most useful and efficient institutions they operated.

We also worked with Hull House, which was located in our area. At this time Hull House had established a community relations department, a project which, I believe, had been set up partly because of the influence of the Chicago Area Project. Under the sponsorship of this department, two small neighborhood centers were started and operated by the parents and a staff of neighborhood leaders who were made available by the Works Project Administration. This department carried on community work, such as encouraging adult groups to take action in legislative matters affecting housing and child welfare problems.

When one day a child cut its foot on a sidewalk strewn with garbage and broken bottles, the parents at one of the neighborhood centers became incensed and decided to take action. But they were calmed down by Bert Boerner, then director of this community relations department and by Joe Giunta, one of our indigenous workers. They suggested they do something constructive about this problem: it was proposed that the parents purchase some old 55-gallon oil drums which, by cutting out the tops, could be made to serve as garbage receptacles. This was done by the parents in one block, and soon the idea spread. Other parents and landlords became interested, and before long a clean-up committee was formed.

This actually took place just before our community committee had been organized, but the Area Project made available a fund of $100 to the committee which it used to set up a revolving fund for the purchase of discarded oil drums to be sold at cost, 30¢ or 40¢ apiece, to tenants and landlords. The cooperation of the ward superintendent of streets and alleys (Vito Marzullo, now alderman of the 25th Ward) was soon enlisted in this project, and he agreed to paint the oil drums and stencil them "20th Ward" and "Keep Our City Clean." The clean-up committee did such a flourishing business that it was soon necessary to hire a horse and wagon to deliver the garbage receptacles.

It was at about this time that we organized our community committee and entered into a close working relationship with Hull House. Since we had a fund of $1,700 from the Area Project for community work, our committee agreed to help the two neighborhood centers to defray some of the expenses of a ward-wide clean-up campaign, the goal being to make available 5,000 garbage receptacles or "a garbage can for every home." Working with Hull House, we broadened the clean-up committee into a coordinating council which included representatives of over 50 social agencies, churches, schools, civic organizations, and clubs, with headquarters at our community committee's office. I was the chairman of this council.

We dramatized this project by using posters, conducting essay contests in schools, and driving a soundtruck around to urge the people to buy garbage cans. Publicity in the community newspapers and the metropolitan press soon said, "If it can be done in the 20th Ward, it can be done anywhere." Soon after, other wards in the city launched similar campaigns in their districts.

We promoted this drive for approximately three years and met our goal. During this period the program was directed by Joseph Giunta, one of our members who at first was employed by the Area Project and later by the Department of Streets and Alleys, though functioning as a representative of our community committee.

During this period we continued working with Hull House in various ways. Its staff members were available to us whenever we needed advice or technical assistance. Our committee, in turn, stimulated community interest in the work which Hull House carried on. We would work jointly in bringing together adults and neighborhood groups to participate in a variety of programs—forums, rallies, community meetings, and special gatherings.

This close working relationship was so effective that before long the community relations department of Hull House was disbanded. Our West Side Community Committee became, in a real and vital sense, Hull House's community relations department. In Chapter 8, I will discuss how we worked jointly with Hull House on a long-range program for the physical reconstruction of the Near West Side.

SETTING UP OUR OWN HEADQUARTERS

Cooperation with our neighborhood institutions and agencies was a good beginning and a constructive effort which continues to this day. But we wanted to establish our own structure and our own identity in a tangible manner. In 1939 we therefore decided to open an office in a storefront on Polk Street near Miller Street. We painted our name on the large windows—West Side Community Committee—and got into action.

At first many of our neighbors likened our function to that of the social and athletic club, because there was no other pattern or symbol for our kind of enterprise. People thought we must be getting together for our own personal benefit for social and recreational activities. We had to keep publicizing and interpreting our work until, in time, the idea took root.

As we started to render services to our neighbors and to make available additional facilities, our work became a well-known and established means of solving personal, family, and neighborhood problems. Shortly after we opened our doors, hundreds of persons started to come to us seeking aid and advice in connection with such matters as old-age pensions, employment, citizenship papers, social security, veterans' problems, notary service, school placements, court appearance, and many other matters which will be discussed in the following chapters.

Our community committee continues to offer this type of service to this day. Since we are literally and figuratively on the ground floor, people naturally turn to us first. Many persons need aid in interpreting their problems to "some agency downtown," or they may want us to accompany them to the Department of Immigration and Naturalization at the "big post office," where they feel lost and confused. Thus a function of our committee is to interpret the work of social agencies and help to make their resources more readily accessible to our people.

Some of us met informally every day at our community committee headquarters and talked about the needs of our children and our community. Every other Friday night regular meetings were held and our subcommittees reported on the problems encountered or the progress made. Here we discussed and formulated those things we deemed desirable for the well-being of our community. Here the people of our community could express their opinions, present suggestions, or voice grievances on matters affecting our common welfare.

At times our meetings took on the character of a debating society, and at times the amount of debating seemed to exceed the amount of work. This was the slow, laborious process which is inherent in democratic procedures. Individual differences and conflicts had to be dealt with, and opposing interests reconciled. Through the medium of these discussions we would ultimately arrive at decisions which became group agreements and plans of the organization as a whole.

Here we learned parliamentary procedures, organizational techniques, and methods of trying to solve problems. Here we had a training ground for young men who wished to develop their abilities to speak and to think with others, so that in time they could become lawyers, doctors, social workers, businessmen, or better parents. As we had hoped, this has since happened to a remarkable degree. Many of us have moved on in the world. From a poor, meagerly equipped Italian boy, I have been honored and dignified by the many tasks and responsibilities it has been my good fortune to assume. Many other friends in this enterprise have developed into outstanding leaders and good citizens.

The die was cast. We had built a solid foundation for our community enterprise so that we could now move ahead. Even if we had solved no basic social problems, our minds and hearts had been changed.

Not long after, we started to see a ray of light flickering over the horizon of our community. We could see something new and bright now. Slowly but surely, our lives were becoming less drab and more interesting. We felt encouraged and pleased with some of our accomplishments, and our despair and uncertainty over the future was being replaced with a new found spirit of faith, hope, and confidence in ourselves, in our community, and in our country.

Here are some comments made by the late Howard Vincent O'Brien after he visited the Near West Side and talked with a number of community residents. It is an excerpt from Mr. O'Brien's then well-known column, "All Things Considered" in the *Chicago Daily News,* which appeared on the eve of the presidential election in 1940:[41]

Odd as it must seem, my thoughts, on the eve of this, the most critical election in our history, are elsewhere. They are in a rather ill-favored corner of my city, a region of mean houses and crowded streets and great poverty; a region where crime and violence used to flourish; a dark region, "bloody," the adjective that policemen and newspaper reporters used to use in describing it—hardly a region in which to seek faith and hope. Yet this is where I found faith and hope, as I never found them in the oratory of politicians. This is where I found democracy in full bloom.

The roots seem to have germinated in a schoolboy club. There, a group of Italo-Americans talked themselves into an idea almost without precedent in these days when people talk so much of "security" and "safety." The idea was to make the place where they lived a better place, and to do it themselves.

They formed what they called a Community Committee and rented a vacant store as a base of operations. They were helped by the Chicago Area Project and by the Institute for Juvenile Research. The help wasn't much, financially—their first year's budget was only $2,000. This group is nonpolitical, nonsectarian. All kinds of young men are in it—and young women too. Among them I met an automobile dealer, a lawyer, a teamster, a school teacher with a doctor's degree from the University of Chicago. Also I met a . . . but let me postpone telling what he was until I have told you how he got there.

He had been a very poor boy and had had little or no schooling. He became a "juvenile delinquent." His probable future was all too plainly "anti-social." No psychiatrist, he. But he does understand human nature. "People want different things," he says. "But there's one thing everybody wants. What everybody wants is attention. For a poor kid like me, one way to get attention was having run-ins with the cops. That made me a big shot to the other kids. Then those guys gets hold of me. They fills me full of hooey. They make me think I'm a different kind of a big shot. They put me to work. When I was in the rackets I didn't work. Now I work nights." This young man is now—of all things—a truant officer! That's the sort of thing the committee has done.

The sociologist would call this "localism." It aims at getting teachers and public servants who grew up with the people among whom they work and who understand racial and religious problems because they have lived with them. Most of all, it is a movement from the bottom up; an answer to the notion that has gained so much headway among Americans, that progress must proceed from the top down.

It is the reason I face the elections so lightly. To me, Roosevelt and Wilkie are much less important than Pete Scalise and Jim Serpe and Lonny Lonigro and Joe (whose last name I can't spell) and those other lads I talked to. As long as there are such Americans the Republic is safe.

Ever since we were encouraged by Howard Vincent O'Brien's story, we tried with even greater zeal and determination to improve conditions in our community and provide more adequate opportunities for our children.

Early in our history our committee operated two small storefront neighborhood centers in addition to our headquarters, also a storefront. These centers were partly subsidized by our parish church, and each was managed by a committee composed of parents and other interested adults who resided near the center. These adults met regularly to discuss the welfare of their children and to make plans for providing various activities. Game rooms, scouting, art work, handicraft, sewing, and various social and athletic events were available for children and young people under the leadership of volunteer leaders and paid workers. Located in the midst of the children's street environment and having the approval and support of parents, these centers exercised a constructive influence on children.

Not only were these centers used for children's activities but they were neighborhood meeting places for adults as well, for parties, baptismals, bridal showers, and other

occasions. During a campaign to stimulate church attendance, a neighborhood center committee had the children
congregate at the center on Sunday morning and with
pomp and ceremony would march them to church. The
children would then return to the center for breakfast.

Here is an example of how parents who were confronted with problem children would call at these centers
for assistance. It appeared in an article on the Chicago Area
Project in *Harper's Magazine*. [42]

> One of these centers, on Garibaldi Place [this street disap-
> peared in the late 1960s, swallowed up by urban renewal] is
> a two-room building formerly used as a store, heated by a
> kerosene stove, with bare floors, a few folding chairs, a desk
> for the program director, a sink, a ping-pong table, and an
> assortment of such games as checkers and parcheesi for
> recreation, and patriotic emblems and war posters for wall
> decorations. Into this place one day recently a mother
> brought her son Jim, a boy of about fourteen who had been
> transferred to a school for truants and incorrigibles. Jim,
> blue-eyed and light-complexioned, in contrast to the Italian
> children who were whooping in the back room, regarded the
> program director with a bland skepticism beyond his years.
> His mother seemed anxious to discuss Jim's incorrigibility,
> but the program director discouraged her, welcomed Jim,
> and sent him into the back room.
>
> It seemed that Jim's main difficulty was that he didn't
> like to be in school or at home. He would disappear for days
> at a time—once he was gone nine days and nobody, not even
> the police, could find him—and when he came back he
> would say only that he had been to a show. Since this seemed
> an inadequate explanation, his mother was haunted by the
> fear so common in this neighborhood that her boy had been
> out robbing. Significantly, she had come for help to the
> Committee's center instead of to the police or the school
> principal, who perhaps already had failed. When the center
> closed for supper at 5:30, the program director talked to
> Jim; so did the president of the West Side Community Com-
> mittee, who happened to drop in on his way home from
> work.
>
> "I hear you like shows, Jim," the program director said.

"Yes."

"You go to shows a lot?"

"Yes," Jim was answering blandly. Surprisingly, he was not trying to avoid his questioner's gaze. Nor did he appear to resent the questioning.

"How often do you go? Couple of times a week?"

"Yes. About that."

"You go straight home from the show?"

"Not always. I haven't for the last five days."

"Where do you go for five days?"

"Oh, lots of times I go down to the Field Museum." (This is located two and a half miles away, a long trip for a West Side boy, for many residents of this area never leave the immediate neighborhood.)

"You can't go to the Field Museum at night."

"Oh no. Daytimes. I work at nights."

"What do you do?"

"I work for the papers. Tribunes, Suns. Downtown."

"You sell them at night?"

"Oh no. Till maybe two o'clock."

"Then where do you go?"

"Oh, maybe I walk around, or maybe I go to my boy-friend's house. Places like that."

"When do you sleep?"

"In the daytime, maybe. In shows. Sometimes I don't sleep."

Jim said his mother intended to make him quit selling papers but he didn't want to. The Committee president, who has no children of his own, said, "Maybe we could find you a job. As a messenger boy, maybe. In a five and dime. Would you like that, Jim?"

"That'd be swell," Jim said. There was genuine eagerness in his voice.

"But only after school. What's the matter with you and school?"

"I don't like Montefiore" (an institution for incorrigibles). He said it was too far from home, too strict; the kids were too tough. He spoke judiciously of the five or six schools he had attended, in the manner of a "college bum." Curiously, he disliked one because the teachers blamed the mothers for the children's truancy; Jim said it was the fault of the teachers and the children themselves. The men said

they would see what they could do toward getting him transferred from Montefiore. He said, "I'd promise anything to
get out of there." (Nobody had asked him to promise anything; this practice, rather common among social workers
and apparently already known to Jim, is considered ineffec-
tual by Shaw's workers.) Jim also said he played hooky because his old shoes embarrassed him. The men offered to
get him a new pair. He seemed interested in swimming at the
"Y" and in joining a Boy Scout Troop (but doubted if he
would have the $15 for a uniform). The program director
invited him to return that evening but he said he thought he
might have to take his little brother to the show if he could
get a dime. Though the questions asked him might seem
about what one would expect from any social worker, that
they were well received because they were asked by a local
ex-delinquent is apparent in the fact that Jim did return that
evening, though he left for the show, alone, after a half-
hour. And, voluntarily, he spent all the next evening at the
center.

In later years, because of changes brought about by
urban renewal, we decided to discontinue these subcen-
ters, but they were an important part of our enterprise in
its earlier years. Other groups about to undertake similar
community ventures would be well advised to consider that
organization in small neighborhood units furnishes residents a common place for meeting and concerning themselves with the needs of their children, increases the base
of participation in a community organization, and frequently provides the occasion and the stimulus for concerted, dramatic action on a community-wide basis.

It is interesting to note that during the past decade
many social agencies which discontinued operating large
settlement houses and community centers have operated
storefront centers, following the pattern used by the community committees affiliated with the Chicago Area Project.
Even some law-enforcement agencies have experimented
with this: police departments, city agencies, and many federally and state-funded poverty projects have decided that

there could be better delivery of their services at the grass-roots level by operating with storefront centers.

While such units are at least located closer to the people, where the problems exist, many are still superimposed —that is, managed and operated by an outside agency. Neighborhood centers of the type our committee has operated, including its present headquarters at 628 South Racine Avenue, are indigenous—funded, managed, and administered by local residents. Because they embody the interests and leadership of the residents, they are likely to exercise greater influence and have more significance in the lives of the people.

Chapter 4

THE CHILD AND THE SCHOOL

Remembering our own difficulties in school, we felt that the school would be another good place to begin our work. The following story illustrates some of the problems we faced.

A Troublemaker's Own Story

My parents came to this country shortly after 1900, and they settled on the Near West Side of Chicago. My mother often related to me that if she had known she was going to stay in this country for the rest of her life she would never have come—not because she didn't like America, but it was leaving her family, her mother and father, sisters and brothers. She thought she was just coming here for a trip and then go back to Italy. However, they settled in a three-room apartment, if you can call it that, on the Near West Side.

My father and mother were uneducated, because, due to the poor circumstances that they had in Italy, they had no chance for schooling. My father got a job at the railroad as a track laborer, struggling on a dollar and a half a day, or whatever the wages were at that time.

A few years later I was born, for better or for worse. The years went by and I got to be about four or five years old. Being the only child, I was kept more or less at home under the close supervision of my mother, thus retarding my ability to speak English. Whatever words I knew were Italian. This is something I don't regret today because it has helped me tremendously in my particular field. [He later became a successful insurance salesman]. I had no playmates, so, when I went out I went with my mother and father. Occasionally, my dad would take me to Lincoln Park and similar places for rides on the street car or the elevated train. Wherever we went, I was always in the company of my father.

Then came the time when I was registered in school. From the first day that I went to school I wanted to run away, because before that I had not been in the company of other children, so everything seemed strange. As a matter of fact, when I registered in school I was taken there by my uncle. He had been here a few years before my folks and he had acquired some knowledge of the English language, so he was delegated to register me in school.

I was afraid of the teacher, the principal, and everybody connected with the school. [Another boy said, "We didn't have any Italian teachers. I think things would have been different if we did."] So, one day at recess I went home and my mother asked me what I was doing home, and I told her I didn't like to go to school—that I preferred staying home.

As time went by I got into first and second grade, and we began to read and write, and our teacher would tell us to study our first grade readers, arithmetic, and stuff like that at home. But, while the other children had brothers and sisters who helped them with their work, I didn't have anybody. Naturally, I couldn't ask my folks to help me with my schoolwork, so I had to strive and struggle on my own. And when we got to school the next morning, the teacher would ask who studied their lessons, so naturally I would say I did and that my folks helped me, because I didn't like for my teacher to know that my folks couldn't speak, read, or write English. I felt kind of funny about that.

With all these handicaps I managed to stay alongside of my classmates and I managed to pass every year with the rest of my class, never failing because of poor schoolwork. But, when we got into fifth grade, I made acquaintances with my neighbor's children who were in the same room, and we had the playground right next to the school. At recess or at lunchtime we would go across the street and pick up cigarette butts, and we soon acquired the habit of smoking. Not being able to buy cigarettes, we used to have what we called "butt partners"; in other words, whoever had a cigarette would give his so-called pal the butt so he would be able to smoke, too.

One day our teacher smelt tobacco on our breath and, finding our shirt pockets stuffed with some fairly good-sized butts that we had picked up, she sent us down to the principal's office. The principal was a stern man at that time, although in later years he sort of adapted himself to the community. He took me into his office and gave me a pretty good thrashing, something that I always held against him while I was going through school. I vowed that some day I would get even with him, which eventually I did.

Due to this incident it seemed that word got around from teacher to teacher that my particular group was a group to be watched—that we were bad. I always felt that the teacher held it against us. And as we were passed from one grade to another the teachers were always on the lookout for our particular group. It got to be a nip-and-tuck battle. Our teachers were of old Irish descent and, for some reason or other, we could see they sort of disliked the Italian kids. They were out to see what they could do with us, either by speaking to us or by beating the hell out of us. In most cases it was the latter.

One day in the seventh grade, Miss O'Hearn, one of the teachers who had a reputation for knocking some of the boys down, came to me and slapped me with a ruler across my right ear. Well, when she did this I got up and took the ruler away from her. Right away she started to run.

That evening after school the word got around that I chased the teacher—especially her—around the room. "Boy if I would of caught her"—that was the word. That established me more with the boys that I was paling around with. This incident led to another visit to the principal and another episode of nip-and-tuck battle. He locked me in a dark little room with him—and him with the yardstick. I managed to get the stick away from him, and he got the bad end of the deal.

So he sent for my parents and threatened to send me to the Montefiore School for problem boys because I was a bad influence on the other children of the school. But we got straightened out, and he gave me another chance. This time his technique was different. He said, "How come such a bright boy, such an intelligent boy causes all the trouble for the school"? He said if I would direct my energies toward the good things I could accomplish much more, but I didn't care what he said and I couldn't see his way, because I had grown to really dislike him tremendously.

Shortly after this teacher incident we were in the art room, and the art teacher was a pal of the seventh-grade teacher. I was caught whispering with a girl, and she said, "Do you think I am going to tolerate this in my room?" She gave me a slap. Well, from chasing the other teacher around the room it must of given me some wind, because this teacher I caught up with. They sent me down again to the principal.

By this time he was really disgusted with me, and he thought that the woodshop teacher, at that time quite a strong fellow, could do something with me. So he sent me to see him. My introduction to him was a nice kick in the pants. The closest thing to me happened to be a mallet and I threw that mallet at him. But I missed.

By this time I had quite a record and reputation in school that I was no good. So I think they tried a new psychology on me: by giving me some responsibility in school maybe I would change. So they made me a bell boy, that is, to ring the bell when school was to begin and when school was let out, and also a supply boy. But by this time I was so bitter towards all these teachers and the principal that it didn't make any difference what responsibilities they gave me. I was set to get even with all of them.

One day as the principal was going home, several of the boys caught him in the schoolyard as he was getting into his car and almost hit him. The only thing that stopped us was when he said that he would have us arrested for trying such a thing. So we let him go. The next day he sent for me again and he expressed his surprise over such a thing. He didn't think that he deserved that. However, he would call the police the next time he heard anything that we had done wrong.

One night several of the boys and I got together right near the school and we began talking about how oppressed and persecuted we were. One of the fellows said, "How's about breaking into the school and really tear the joint down?" That was all right with all of us. So I said, "I don't care what you fellows do. I just want to go into the principal's office."

We broke in, and it seemed that everyone had a grievance against his own teacher. We went into the office first and got the keys to several of the rooms, and we just tore everything up, turned the tables over, spilled ink, and damaged the furniture—whatever we thought would really hurt the principal and some of these teachers. The damage was quite expensive. I think it was about $180.

The next morning word got around that someone had broken into the school. There were all sorts of stories—How many typewriters had been stolen, this and that, but none of them was true. So one of the fellows was picked up and I was too. They began questioning us as to what we knew about the vandalism that had occurred the previous night. They couldn't pin anything on us, so we got away with it.

The problems described here existed during the 1920s. By the late 1930s, family and community life had become more stable, and conflicts between the school and the community were not so acute as they had been.

Reaching the School Principal

To our immigrant parents, the school was an alien institution. It was run by Irish teachers who were complete strangers to the community; a school was merely a place to send children during the day so they could learn to read and write. The six public schools in our area in the 1930s were huge, three-story structures that seemed to blend in with the nearby factories and industries. They appeared cold and impersonal. The three Catholic parochial schools and the "Greek school" were closer to our parents' experiences, since they were church-related and hence an integral part of the community.

Very few of our parents ever had occasion to visit the public school; they usually went there only when called in by the principal to discuss the misbehavior of a child. When this happened, communication problems usually led to more confusion and conflict. There was always a serious problem, for example, when a principal wanted to get rid of a problem boy by transferring him to a special school for the "socially maladjusted."

One time I suggested to the principal that a boy should be given a chance to tell why he was misbehaving in school. The principal was shocked by what he took to be a questioning of his authority. Even if the boy was right, he held, the authority of the school was supreme and could not, should not, be questioned.

But one of a child's problems may be that the people he lives with do not respect the authority of the school or other agencies; if so, that authority may be ineffective, if not downright damaging. The most effective authority arises out of the common understanding and consensus of the people of the community. A school that operates independently of, or in conflict with, the community is not likely to achieve a high degree of success in coping with the needs of the child. In such a situation, the child is more likely to rebel against the authority imposed by the school.

To one of our meetings we invited the principal of the school from which I had graduated, the Andrew Jackson Elementary School. This man, as I said before, had been serving in the capacity of school principal for over ten years, and during this time he had never spent one evening in the neighborhood. As far as we knew, our invitation was the first he had ever received from a local group. When he met with us, he was amazed and impressed. Present in our group were young men who had been some of the leading truants and delinquents in the school. He recognized faces of men who had been rowdy, mischievous, and incorrigible boys—boys who had thrown snowballs at teachers, boys who had broken windows, boys who had raided the school and had done unmentionable things. (Today, they can be mentioned. From a life history on file at the Institute for Juvenile Research: "After school I met the gang and they knew of course who burglarized the school and we all got a big kick out of it and were saying, 'That old mother-fucker, I'll bet he got sick when he seen that shit on his desk.' " Albert Cohen has written, "There is an element of active spite and malice, contempt and ridicule, challenge and defiance, exquisitely symbolized in an incident described to the author by Mr. Henry D. McKay, of defecating on the teacher's desk."[43])

The very fact that such a group could come together to carry on civic work was in itself an astounding accomplishment to him. He was delighted to be with us, and he encouraged us. When we asked him if there were immediate problems confronting him in the management of the school, he asked for our assistance in dealing with several situations that were jeopardizing the welfare of our school-children. He told us that the engineer-custodian was a habitual drunkard, an incompetent and senile political job-holder who should have long since been retired. The principal reported that the school building was inadequately heated, that repairs on the school plant were badly needed, and that the engineer was negligent in the maintenance of the building. Although the principal had sent in complaints to the board of education, no action had ever been taken.

We immediately appointed a school committee, and the following day a group of five men visited the school and acquainted themselves with the situation. The school was not adequately heated, and the building was in need of paint and repairs. When we called on the school engineer at his office, we were first greeted by an attendant who looked us over suspiciously. After some delay we were admitted to a small office.

As we came in, we were assailed by the stench of alcohol. It was apparent that the engineer-custodian had been drinking. He proceeded to tell us how capable and efficient he was, but he was a pathetic sight. He frothed at the mouth, and his eyes had a lazy, listless look, hardly the countenance befitting a school engineer. He muttered something in his defense to the effect that he knew all the boys around the barbershop, Joe and Mike and Paul. It was obvious that he was a hopeless case, so we departed determined to take the necessary action to have him replaced by a competent person.

We called and wrote to the chief engineer at the offices of the board of education demanding that this incompetent be transferred from the school. Meanwhile we reported to our members and spread the word around the neighborhood regarding the existing situation, indicating that we might need the assistance of all the parents. In less than a week the engineer-custodian was replaced by a younger, more vigorous and alert man. Shortly after, when a PTA was organized at this school, we had a committee of mothers call on the new engineer and express their appreciation for having a conscientious person on the job. They told him of the unfortunate experience with his predecessor and assured him that they were confident he was well qualified for his new job.

Another problem that the principal suggested we try to tackle was broken windows in the school building. The school developed an unusually large number of broken windows in the course of a year. We suggested that we enlist the interest and cooperation of the parents. Together with the principal we planned a special program and invited 100 mothers, most of whom lived opposite the school building. The children provided an hour of entertainment, followed by refreshments contributed by some of the mothers.

When the meeting got underway, several of the mothers spoke up: "We certainly enjoyed being here today." "This is the first time I have been in this school." "The last time I was here was five years ago when my boy was in trouble." "You know, I didn't realize our children could perform so well." "I think it would be wonderful if we could meet like this more often."

These were genuine, spontaneous comments. But in addition we had our lobbyists and propagandists well represented. One of them said, "Well, how about organizing a PTA here—other schools have them." The principal said that there are two kinds of PTAs: good ones and bad ones. If a PTA cooperated amicably with the principal and teachers, it could be an asset to the school. He said he hadn't thought too much about the idea and had some doubts about whether one could function successfully in this neighborhood. However, since there now seemed to be some community interest he was willing to give this program a chance. Years later, when an active and useful organization was well established, he confessed to us that he was almost sure at first that the group would fail due to lack of interest by parents.

The next month a similar meeting was called, and representatives of the district PTA council were invited to acquaint the people with the objectives and scope of the PTA. A month later the group was formally organized, officers were elected, and about 60 members paid their annual dues. The PTA had become a going concern. The first president, Mrs. Lucile Tricarico, was an aggressive, articulate young mother who had graduated from the school herself and now had two children in it. This was the first PTA in our community.

After several years there were 286 members, representing about 75 percent of the parents who had children in this school. A year after the PTA was organized, the principal reported that few windows had been broken. Ordinarily the number of broken windows in the course of one year was astronomical.

Another innovation was the use of the school assembly hall for evening functions. Heretofore the building had never been open after 3:15 for neighborhood use. The PTA staged special assembly programs, three a year, so that working parents could attend and become acquainted with their school. Admissions were charged to some of these events, and the proceeds were used to buy raincoats for the patrol boys, eyeglasses for needy children, books for the school library, and for similar purposes.

DIARIES OF TRUANT OFFICERS

We decided to take a further step by suggesting to the board of education that two of our young men be employed as truant officers. With the help of the Chicago Area Project, we soon succeeded in having Paul D'Arco and Samuel Serpe, two college graduates, assigned as truant officers in our community.

This practice of making personnel available to the school at the request of the people of the community, not some vested interest, was absolutely without precedent. These truant officers were selected by our community organization, and their assignment was made possible because of our interest in having local young men function as agents of the people, with interests and loyalties to the whole community. The beneficial psychological effect this had on our people was readily observed, as a truant officer's diary reveals:

> The most evident response to an appointment of a local person to the position of truant officer is one of surprise.

"It's about time our boys get up in the world," some said. Others indicated surprise that anyone could possibly enjoy being a truant officer. "Do you like that work?" was a question frequently asked at first. However, in general the entire community is definitely pleased with the local truant officers. One very important benefit of this situation is the greater occasion for understanding between the truant officer and the parents, once the language difficulty is removed. Since many of the parents speak only their native tongue, much of the relationship between the school and the home can be discussed in more factual manner.

The effect these truant officers had on the children also seemed to be beneficial. As Paul notes, "One day I was sitting in the West Side Community Committee office when two youngsters passed by and one called across the open door: 'Hey, are you the truant officer now?' To which I answered, 'Yes.' 'You can't be,' the boy said in a pleased and amazed tone of voice."

These excerpts from truant officers' diaries are not quoted to criticize the teachers or the schools. They worked assiduously for many years to teach and train our children. We knew that they had had an exceedingly difficult task and were certainly not to be blamed for the shortcomings and failures of our families and our community.

Teachers naturally found it extremely difficult to teach in our community. Coming as they did from middle-class homes, they evaluated their success in the framework of middle-class values and were frustrated when they found themselves unable to deal with children on this level. A wide cultural gulf existed between these teachers and the school and most people of our community. Obviously the teachers and parents found it almost impossible to be cooperative agents in educating the child.

Paul's diary contains this statement: "During the first week of my work as truant officer, one of the teachers told me: 'I think you have a pretty tough job going after all those tough kids. I certainly don't envy you.' I replied: 'On the other hand I think you have a harder job. You've got to be in there on the job all day long teaching a large class, which is not an easy task!' To this she replied: 'Well, you may be right at that; at least you don't have to smell them all day long.' "

The diary cites another teacher's reaction: "In the same school Mr. S. was discussing one of his truant cases and said, 'Why bother about the whole thing? I expect to see Bob's name in the headlines some of these days. He will probably be one of our big hoodlums here.' Another teacher in the second grade told the truant officer that she hoped the 'dumb kids' would stay home. One boy reported that his teacher called him down because he answered her back with a silly remark and she said, 'You are so silly you would laugh at your own mother's funeral.' "

For one thing, our truant officers did not function as the truant officer of years past, who had been used by the school as a bogeyman to intimidate kids and pull them into the school with no understanding of their behavior difficulties. The situation our men operated in was quite different. First of all, they had been born and raised in the community and had intimate contacts with many persons and groups. Secondly, they established an office out in our community headquarters in addition to their posts in the school. Being right on the ground floor, literally and socially, they were thus identified as agents of the community, not representatives of an impersonal, far-removed institution.

Here the people could come without hesitation to reveal their woes. Here children could come voluntarily or at the truant officer's invitation to talk things over, to give vent to some dissatisfaction. Here parents could call in the evening at their convenience to discuss problems. In this informal neighborhood situation, some of the basic problems of the school were revealed.

The diary goes on:

The teachers in two of the six public elementary schools in our areas want me to "scare" the children into attending school, always holding Parental School or the Montefiore Special School as clubs over their heads. I noticed that Mrs. S. did this often. One day as she was ranting about the action she would take with truants, one of the boys began to cry in fear of what might happen.

Mrs. D. said that the teacher embarrasses her daughter by calling her down before the whole class. Mrs. D. rightfully stated, "Why can't she talk to her privately and explain things to her?"

Mrs. S. accused a teacher of calling her children brats. Mrs. M. complained that a certain teacher called her children "nothing but a bunch of morons," and a child was told by the teacher, "You're going to get a N if you don't bring any crayons." Mrs. M. says that these children aren't bad, but treating the children that way makes them bad. (This family is on relief and buying crayons isn't the easiest thing for them.)

Another mother was exasperated about the teacher's attitude toward her child:

Mrs. C. remarked to me one day when we were talking about her boy who had been having difficulties about staying in school regularly, "You know what it is; he is afraid to go back. The teachers holler at him. If they could talk nice to him and try to help him, they would get along better. The first thing they say to him is, "Bring your mother, bring your mother." If I can't go, then the boy can't go to school. I can't leave my house just like that anytime. I have a lot of things to do at home." This last remark points out one of the minor causes of truancy; in at least two other cases children have stayed home until such time as their parents were able to accompany them back. Some parents work, and that complicates the matter much more.

Our truant officers discovered other practices and attitudes that seemed to contribute to children's behavior difficulties and truancy. In several instances teachers were coercing children in various ways. A mother reported about a parochial school: "Once in a while my girl used to be late in bringing the tuition, and the sister used to say to her she wouldn't be promoted if she didn't bring it. Every time it would be the same story. My poor girl used to feel so bad she almost got sick over it. She lost so much weight that year."

The truant officer notes: "This practice of using promotion to coerce children into activity is quite common in both public and parochial schools."

The problem of our retarded children was not handled with much sympathy or understanding in some of our schools. Some principals evaded the responsibility entirely, as the following example will indicate. Marvin, 13 years old, was attending the ungraded division at the X school until Mr. Z., the principal, abolished this special room. Consequently Marvin and 15 other pupils were transferred to another school about six blocks away, which required crossing two dangerous intersections. The father, who was in delicate health, wanted his son to continue going to the same school close to his home, but since it was discovered by the child study department of the board of education that he had an IQ of 67, he had to continue in an ungraded division.

In the new school situation, Marvin, along with other children, frequently was struck across the head and shoulders with a fat stick. Our truant officer found that the teacher of this room had no control over the pupils and revealed her incompetence by her attitude toward Marvin. One day she said that it would be better for him to stay home since he was not learning much and after all, "That guy looks like a moron." When the boy's father spoke to our truant officer about his possible transfer to a school closer to his home, the principal told him to "drop the case and let the father take care of his own boy."

Poverty problems frequently made it very difficult for children to attend school. One mother wrote to a principal, "I have one daughter in school and one at home who is now old enough to go to school. I would like very much to send her to school but she does not have any shoes. They both need shoes very badly and I cannot afford to buy them. My husband does not have a job and we have no money to buy the shoes for my two girls. I want them to go to school. I thank you very much."

Since getting new shoes was a difficult task, our truant officer suggested that the principal should attempt to get a cobbler—who during those relief days were made available through WPA—so that old shoes could be repaired. The principal said that the pupils in the school get enough service the way it is, and she wouldn't want the bother of a cobbler in the school. Fortunately, other principals did not have this same attitude.

The following comment in a truant officer's diary illustrates similar problems and indicates the manner and spirit in which our truant officers worked:

> One day I was driving down Taylor Street when I met a group of boys from the neighborhood on their way back from Creiger. I invited them in and gave them a lift home. Angelo [this is the same boy who is mentioned in Chapter 5] told me about his younger brother, who was going to the X Elementary School and two other fellows who had been ditching that afternoon. This truancy was not reported to · me by the teacher, but I called the three boys into our community office and we talked the thing over. Angelo is only 17 years of age but is one of the boys who stays close to our office pretty regularly. The three truants felt no compunction about coming in and talking the problem over. One of these boys was staying home from school because he didn't have a gym suit. The teacher had told him either to get a suit or get out of the class. This is quite a problem, especially among girls, who also have to buy gym clothes. I talked things over with the boys and they have been attending

school regularly in recent weeks. I discussed their problem
with the adjustment teachers at the school and they tried to
ease matters for the boys.

HUMAN AND INSTITUTIONAL RESOURCES

Thus, by virtue of the personal and social relationships
which our truant officers maintained they were able to establish the proper rapport with children and to get at the
root of the trouble. Our truant officers worked on the theory that only through a thorough understanding of all community factors influencing the child could they begin to
alter the situation constructively and help the child out of
his difficulty. They made deliberate efforts to maintain
close contact with community persons, groups, and institutions that might be significantly related to the children with
whom they dealt. This meant close contact with parents,
priests, and politicians on the one hand, and teachers, principals and social agency workers on the other.

This background of contacts and intimate connections
provided means for solving some of our problems. From all
these sources the truant officers could get a clearer picture
of the influences operating on a given child.

They became identified more closely with the local
parks, settlements, and community centers, whenever possible spending a late afternoon or evening in the game-
room or gymnasium. In this way they tried to link the
problem of the schoolchild with the neighborhood resources which were also trying to meet his needs. One of
the local precinct captains agreed to furnish clothing for
children who were unable to attend school for lack of it.
Similarly, our community committee enlisted the aid of a
local women's club—the Thoughtful Friends Club—in
making available money to purchase shoes for schoolchildren.

In other instances boys were referred to local social and athletic clubs; these would frequently provide information about activities of truants and at the same time would agree to keep an eye on the boys.

In one school our committee was able to interest the principal and the mothers' club in launching a program designed to improve the health of schoolchildren. It was ironic that one of the world's largest medical schools, the University of Illinois Medical School, was only two blocks away from the school, yet one-third of the approximately 1,400 pupils had serious health problems and another third suffered from a variety of less serious physical ailments. Here within our grasp were clinics, hospitals, research facilities, medical schools, and laboratories. Yet they were not being used for the human needs in our backyard. We decided to do something about it.

We invited our local doctors to a meeting at this school to enlist their interest and aid in a program which had been started on a small scale by the physical education instructor at the school. The plan was to carry on a systematic health program for the children, first by having them thoroughly examined at the various clinics in the area, second to do intensive follow-up work on every child who required medical attention.

The doctors responded favorably, as we had hoped. It was obvious to them that this plan would not infringe on their business but instead would actually stimulate it. According to our plan, children were taken in groups to local clinics, accompanied at times by our truant officers. The findings on each child were then discussed with the parents by either the physical instructor or principal of the school, who urged that the parents go to their own physician for the required medical aid. If parents were unable to bear the expense, which they were in the majority of cases, then arrangements were made to have the physical ailment treated in the local clinics.

In the course of two years, practically every child had been given this service. The results were very encouraging. At a later meeting this plan was suggested to all the principals of the other local schools. Some of them, however, had conservative notions about the function of the school and did not wish to take any responsibility for such a task. Another school responded favorably and developed a similar program.

Our committee called on the board of education in an effort to get its permission to carry on a health program of this nature in every school in our community. This would require, as we suggested, the part-time services of one teacher to help on some of the detail work. Because of the financial problems involved, however, the plan was not accepted, so we had to continue doing what we could on a piecemeal basis.

At almost every meeting of our community committee our truant officers would report on the problems they encountered. These problems were then discussed, and efforts were made to cope with them. Some truant and problem children were put on the committee's special "payroll," a small fund set aside to employ them part time as office boys, messengers, or janitors.

We soon learned, however, that we could not cope with all the problems at one time—the problem of negative and biased teacher attitudes, of parent education, of establishing a closer relationship between all the known problem children and constructive community influences, the poor health of schoolchildren, the poverty problem, and so forth. These problems existed in some form or other in our six public and three parochial elementary schools. How to tackle all of these situations with two truant officers burdened as they were with red tape and limited time?

The sheer task of mobilizing all the human and institutional resources of our community and city to deal effectively with these problems would have been a gigantic task.

But we did what we could, wherever and whenever the soil would permit favorable cultivation. Where the principal responded favorably, we organized a parent-teacher association. Where a social agency agreed to work with truant and problem children, we referred them there. Where a social and athletic club or political organization offered to help, we utilized them. The fact that these things could be done on a small scale meant that much more could be done if similar working relationships and methods of operation could be instituted by cooperating organizations.

We worked on this basis for approximately three years, until the events of December 7, 1941. It was then no longer feasible for our truant officers to continue in this capacity because of inadequate salaries, greater attractions in other fields, and because of political and other changes in the administration of the board of education. We continued working closely with our local schools and with the new truant officers who were later assigned to schools in our community.

Generally, our local schools have come to recognize the importance of using neighborhood resources such as those represented in our community enterprise. Calls come frequently to our committee's headquarters from teachers, principals, truant officers, and adjustment teachers for assistance in helping to meet the needs of our schoolchildren.

In addition to these direct services for children, our committee has worked with the schools in other ways. For example, we have presented small trophies to the outstanding pupils of each school every semester, usually at graduation time. This is another medium for us to keep stimulating the interest of our parents in the welfare of children and of the community as a whole. The presentation of these trophies at school assemblies is another example of a simple device encouraging the participation of our people in the affairs of the school. And indeed this is an excellent opportunity for us to dramatize "good" behavior, a practice which sorely needs to be done more often in our society. Unfortunately, our society seems to thrive on the dramatization of evil.

Finally, recently our committee launched an extensive sports program in conjunction with local public and parochial schools. Boys and girls recruited from the schools are organized into teams who compete in a community-wide tournament. Events include baseball, softball, basketball, indoor hockey, and volleyball; all games are played in Sheridan Park, except for the tennis games played in facilities provided by the University of Illinois at Chicago Circle. As this book is going to press, our committee and the Near West Side Conservation Council are negotiating with the Chicago Park District and the Department of Urban Renewal for the construction of a new $3 million fieldhouse and playground.

This extensive sports program is being promoted enthusiastically by Ernest Mategrano, Jr., president of the committee, aided by many volunteers. Most of the equipment for this program is purchased by the committee, as are the numerous awards and trophies presented to the winners.

Chapter 5

FROM GANGS TO CLUBS

We knew from experience that one of the places where delinquency originated was the random and spontaneous play situations of little gangs. Horse play and daredevil tricks turned to breaking windows, tearing out lead pipes from abandoned buildings, or destroying other property. Daring your playmates to take fruit from a passing peddler's wagon was mere "play"—play which frequently started boys on a career of delinquency.

The antisocial gang is not willfully created or formally organized by anyone; it arises and develops as do the cells in organic matter. Just as the biologist cannot ignore the cell, the sociologist cannot ignore the gang and the milieu in which it begins. Instead of trying to organize artificial groups, we sought out the little neighborhood gangs already there and started with them.

The Sheridan Gang

The Sheridan Gang was one of approximately 75 boys' gangs on the Near West Side. We had begun working with it in 1934, when I was employed on the Children's Leisure Time Service, through the West Side Community Council. We knew this group was what was termed an unofficial delinquent gang, although a few members of the group did have official records. The boys who had official court records did not engage in any more delinquency than the boys who did have records, though. Bascially they all played together and occasionally stole together.

It is difficult to say what the future of this gang would have been without our influence, but there's good reason to believe that they would have committed many more serious types of delinquencies had it not been for us. Also, this gang was vaguely aware of the broader efforts of our community work.

My first contact with these dozen gang members was on a cool summer evening when they were sitting around a fire in an empty lot roasting potatoes. Having had such experiences myself, I knew the wood for the fire was probably part of somebody's backyard fence and the potatoes were taken from some local peddler's wagon. But you don't ask questions about such things. You just join them with, "Hello guys, nice fire you have here!"

You tried to be part of their gang in a clumsy sort of way and then interest them in joining the softball tournament which the "club" or the "stable" was sponsoring. "Play ball?" "Sure, when do we start?" was the inevitable reply. Then you had them under your wing. Later on I would take the group to the woods for hikes and picnics and to other places of interest.

In the winter of 1934, arrangements were made with our local pastor to use the parochial school basement for meeting rooms and a social center for our club groups.

This basement served as the game room for our various groups during the winter, and at the same time it gave us an opportunity to be closer to the church, so that gradually we were able to interest the priests in working with us on other welfare projects.

The following summer we introduced our own make-shift camping program. We purchased a discarded newspaper truck, a couple of tents, some pots and pans, and other contraptions used for camping outdoors. This alone was enough to make all the neighborhood kids wild with excitement and eager to go on our camping expeditions to Lake Eliza, near Valparaiso, Indiana, about 60 miles from our neighborhood.

The Sheridan Gang was one of the many groups we took to Lake Eliza for three-day outings. If nothing else, these camping trips made it possible for us to put to good use the government canned beef famous in those relief days. Many families disliked canned meat and never used this "relief beef," as it was called. Since our campers were asked to bring canned goods for their "camp fee," many of them brought this relief beef. Interestingly enough, the boys ate the stuff when dished out as Mulligan stew, a concoction of meat and vegetables colored with tomato sauce. These camping expeditions were soon the talk of the town.

The trip in our novel vehicle, the opportunity to see the countryside, farms, and animals, the scenic campsite overlooking the lake—boating, fishing, campfires, stories, singing—these made a profound impression on the minds and personalities of these boys. Little did we know that most of them were to profit significantly from such experiences, that we were preparing them for expeditions the world over—in the Pacific Islands, in Italy, Germany, and France. And little did we know that some of these boys were to have permanent homes in those far-off places. They departed, never to return to our community: Robert, lying

in the earth of Okinawa; Louis, somewhere in Germany—
and others.

But I especially remember Robert and Louis. Robert
was an assistant of our summer camp while he was on
supervision from our state training school. All too soon he
turned 18 and was inducted into the army. Louis's hobby
and the profession he planned was unique in our community; he was an ardent amateur geologist, just starting in
college when his career was interrupted by the call to arms.

In the spring of 1935 we tried to see whether boys in
our community would respond favorably to the boy scout
program. Scouting had always been conspicuous in our
area for its almost total absence.

> While I was in Parental School I joined the boy scouts,
> figuring they would treat you better and that you get away
> with stuff. We would have a meeting about twice a week and
> the scoutmaster would tell us all different stories. I didn't
> like it. I thought it was a lot of shit. I don't see what anybody
> got out of that. Maybe it was interesting for some kids but
> not for me. (From Life History 58, Institute for Juvenile
> Research)

It was "sissy stuff" for most of our boys, and a scout in
uniform was an oddity. A troop would spring up now and
then in one of our local social settlements under the leadership of a worker, who would usually be the scoutmaster.

But some of us knew that the content of the scouting
program was wholesome and educational and felt that if it
was sponsored by community leaders our boys would take
to it. Since scouting was essentially an outdoor program of
hiking, camping, and nature lore, we knew that our boys
would be enthusiastic about it.

The Chicago Council of Boy Scouts of America was
especially interested in promoting scouting in our community, because it knew that there were few scouts in such
"less chance areas." This contrasted with the districts of

higher economic status, where the activity seemed to be more popular and was supported by the parents and the community. Another reason scouting never took root in our community was because it was, of course, expensive. Many of our boys could not afford the membership fee, the uniform, the camping expenses, and other costs. Some people claimed that many boys could afford such expenses since they readily found money for movies, comics, and similar commercialized recreation. However, the primary reason children in our community had not responded in large numbers to scouting was because it was not an established pattern in our local culture.

It was our feeling that at the outset scouting would have to be subsidized and possibly presented in a modified form. Accordingly, the Chicago Council and the Area Project jointly contributed funds to be used to hire a local worker to get the program started and to help defray some of the expenses which the boys could not or would not meet. I became that worker. By this time the state's Children's Leisure Time Service was liquidated to make way for various federal projects, so I needed other employment. Many of our boys were on relief and the 50¢ fee was a burden; so if a boy was interested we paid his fee from this fund, always attempting to have him pay a small part of it or work out the amount in service to the center.

Within a year we had three troops and a cub pack, with over 200 boys enrolled. Our method of enlisting the boys was to interest a natural play group like the Sheridan Gang. We took this group on hikes and trips, had campfires in empty lots (the boys called them "bomb-fires"), and at the center they were engaged in a variety of activities that did not differ essentially from the activities of the scouting program. At first we used movies at the meetings and set aside a room in the club which belonged to the scouts, who decorated and fixed it up in their own way. Scouting became a regular and established part of the center's program, if not its most popular activity.

The Sheridan Gang was known during this stage as the Wolf Patrol, with Angelo, the most zealous member, as patrol leader. At the beginning several other older members of the group were the recognized leaders, but Angelo was always an influential member of the group. He continued to be the leader of the group long after the members outgrew scouting. Later, when they organized into the Alcoves Social and Athletic Club, he became president of the group.

I recall, however, that at times there were problems in trying to explain the boy scout motto to some of our delinquents. On one occasion, just before he went to the district board to take a test, I explained to Jimmy what it means to "be prepared," but when Jimmy was asked by one of the examiners, he said being prepared meant, "When you go on a heist ya gotta be sure ya have a good car and the right guys. One guy has to be the wheelman, another guy has to be the lookout man, and you gotta have guys with guts to go inside the joint to pull the heist." I don't know whether we ever lived that one down!

Another time the program was in jeopardy when at a summer camp a hard-core delinquent burglarized the commissary and took cash and supplies worth over $100. The camp director wanted to oust our whole group unless we got to the bottom of this offense. When we questioned the boys, Sam confessed, restitution was made, and the camp director was placated.

At the beginning of our camp trips we also had many problems of discipline. Our boys would get into fights with scouts from the middle-class areas. To our boys, the outsiders were "sissies" and "fruits." These attitudes and the profanity the boys used was enough to start quite a few battles.

Some boys, especially the older ones who had never been out in the country, had difficulty adjusting to the great outdoors. I remember on one trip a few hours after we arrived, Albert came up to me and said, "I wanna go home.

Nothing to do here. No pool, no cards. To goddamn quiet here for me." He missed the sounds, noises, smells, and action of the city streets, and while he stuck it out for the week, I could see that he was happy to get back to Taylor Street.

Corner Boys Go Indoors

Our experience had clearly been that the activities of the boys' club, settlements, or community centers were not sufficiently exciting to sustain the interests of boys in their teens. At least this seemed to be the case in our community. These boys went to agencies for occasional gym classes or showers, but at this age they were not interested in ping-pong or craft shops or singing in classes. Pulled by the influences of the streets, they became street corner boys, interested in billiards, bowling, skating, cards, and most of all, girls, sex, and dancing. A big emphasis was placed on cars and clothes—being a "smart dresser." It was difficult for a social agency to compete with the attractions flaunted in movies, newspapers, magazines, and radio (and nowadays on television). The luxury patterns of these urban institutions exert powerful influences on the values and personalities of boys in their formative years, as they do on all of us regardless of age.

As already indicated, such groups emerged in the natural course of events in the lives of young men in our community. These young men spontaneously created their own little societies, as man has always done, to satisfy the basic human need for association and communication with other human beings. The individual always strives for participation and acceptance in some group. He seeks association and fellowship with people who will receive him on an equal basis and give him the opportunity to express himself. The social and athletic clubs in our community met just such vital needs. They had appeared without guidance or supervision by any welfare agency.

Following the career of Angelo and his gang, we can describe the origin and development of a specific social and athletic club and indicate how such clubs operated and served the needs of their members. When Angelo and his boys grew out of scouting, stopped attending the Community Center regularly, and were spending most of their time on the streets, other members of the committee and I remained in contact with them, so they knew firsthand of our efforts to develop the community committee. A serious effort to establish their own storefront club began. They were not able in the beginning to finance the project, so they met in an old shack.

Further efforts to develop the club were interrupted shortly afterwards by the onset of World War II, which automatically inducted most of these young men into the armed forces. Even after they went to war, they were kept fully informed of our work through our *Community News,* which was revived in 1944 because Angelo suggested it in a letter from a foxhole in New Guinea.

When these young men returned to civilian life, they naturally got together on the street corners and frequented our community headquarters. With Angelo again as the sparkplug of the group, the boys chipped in a few dollars apiece and rented an empty store which had formerly been a tavern. This was a large room used for meetings, with a small bar and a few booths at one end. The interior was lined throughout with knotty pine, giving the room a rustic atmosphere. The boys started to pick up secondhand furniture, an oil stove, a radio, and a few tables. As the membership increased from about 15 to 25, additional income from the 50¢ weekly dues paid by the members made it possible to secure better furniture and make other improvements. Within a year the group prospered considerably. By this time the group was ready to sponsor its annual dance, an activity which represents the most important social and financial event of the year. This event was anticipated and planned by all members many months before the set date.

Each member was compelled to take and "swallow" an agreed number of tickets, as well as to solicit a number of pages of advertisements for the program book which was published in conjunction with the event—a good source of revenue. When Alcoves SAC sponsored a dance one year in a large local auditorium, it drew a crowd of around 500 young people and netted the group $1,400. With this money the group made other improvements in their club; they had linoleum installed, decorated the quarters, and purchased new furniture.

A keen spirit of competition existed among the numerous social and athletic clubs in the area, each one attempting to outdo the other in the appearance of their club. An effort was made to put up a swanky front as well as neat and comfortable quarters. Each of the storefront windows expressed the ideas and individuality of the club. Some had venetian blinds and neon lights. Indeed, a stranger might have mistaken some of the clubs for fancy cocktail lounges.

The local precinct captain, usually a member of one of these groups or having close contact with key members, performed services for them, recognizing as he did their political possibilities. The precinct captain was always on call if somebody was in trouble and needed help—he had "contacts." He was a booster of these organizations and attempted to secure sweaters or uniforms for their teams by soliciting the assistance of businessmen or other community leaders. In doing all these things the precinct captain, like the politician, was assuring himself a constituency. He worked with the young men as a neighbor on a mutual basis. He knew their lingo and their ways.

In other words, he had his ear to the ground and was usually in a better position than the agency leader to understand the hopes and fears of his constituents. He did not have to resort to home visits in the formal manner of an agency worker: he had his own set of techniques garnered in the college of hard knocks. The agency worker had his techniques, too, but the pity of it is that he was and is usually too far removed from the people to use them effectively for community welfare. Some day we may learn how to combine the skill, shrewdness, and ingenuity of the politician and the abilities and technical knowledge of the welfare worker in community improvement programs. The two are not irreconcilable, as some people think. Their goals are the same—both are interested in the welfare of human beings; so they have a basis for cooperation in a common problem.

Some elements in our community did not always look with favor on these groups. Some social agencies would have preferred them to disband and their members to join settlements and community centers. Some residents were suspicious of their morals and feared the drinking and card-playing which goes on in almost every club.

But criticism of the social and athletic club on moral grounds is not justifiable, in my opinion. With some exceptions, the drinking or gambling which took place in these groups was no more of a problem than elsewhere in the community. The young men got together principally for card-playing and a coke or a bottle of beer, just as they would at home. The members of each of these clubs strove to preserve the reputation which they had earned over the years as athletes and responsible young men. Consequently there was a compulsion toward conformity to the conventional or semiconventional patterns of the community.

With some exceptions: some members violated the rules of the clubs, but an informal machinery for justice operated toward such persons. Violators were fined, warned, or reprimanded, the severity of the treatment depending on the seriousness of the violations. Disapprobation or fear of ostracism from the group was one of the instruments of social control.

Some people contended that these groups were entirely independent and selfish and existed solely to satisfy the interest of the members, thus having no civic or social value to the community. True, these groups were traditionally self-centered, but in meeting the personal and social needs of the members they were indirectly of value to the community in the same way that a stable family, albeit a self-centered one, is of value to the community. Furthermore, the motives of these groups were no different from those of benefit societies, country clubs, associations of commerce, or labor unions. All of them meet together for a common purpose and seek to satisfy certain personal and social objectives.

We consistently encouraged these social and athletic units in our community. Early in our history, during the Depression, it was a policy of our organization to lend financial assistance to such groups by paying the first month's rent, by making a direct contribution for furniture or repairs, or by giving assistance in applying for a charter and drawing up their constitution. When The Tru-Pals SAC started the practice of giving Christmas parties for the children in their immediate neighborhood, our committee contributed money to their effort, encouraged them, and gave them recognition in our community newspaper and in the metropolitan press. As we had hoped, the example of this club gradually was emulated by other groups.

As residents, we regarded these groups as our boys, and we had an open door policy with them. Over the years, with other members of our staff and members of the committee, I worked with these clubs to try to solve problems of employment, education, family, delinquency, and crime.

In a conversation around 1950, Angelo told with pride some of his efforts in assisting a delinquent boy and two young men who were recently discharged from a penitentiary:

I know now what you and the committee were trying to do with me and other guys who used to have a habit of getting in trouble. You encouraged us, worked with us, and stayed with us, appeared in court, took us out of jail, helped us out, never turned against us. You never looked down your nose or felt superior. When we were punks and young squirts we did not know what you were doing, but I suppose unconsciously we were drawn to you. What you did got to be a habit with me, and I'm now trying to do some of the things with some of our guys in the club.

Take Jimmy—he was a tough punk, or thought he was. He was always acting smart and stealing, and he thought he was going to be a big hood. When he started to hang around our club, some of the guys tried to push him out, said he was too young, too smart-alecky. So I stuck up for him and said, "Look here, Jimmy, if you want to belong to this club, wipe that smart look off your face and go along, see?" Jimmy is now quite a changed guy. That put-on tough look is gone, and he worked hard to be a good member. He is the youngest guy we have, and being with us older guys makes him feel big.

Angelo went on to tell of another chap:

You remember Jack. He was what you positively call a delinquent. He was always stealing and fooling around and could never be straightened out by his family. While he was in the army he went AWOL and went on a binge which landed him in the army prison for several years. When he came out and started to hang around with us, the guys didn't warm up to him. They were mostly all veterans and didn't want anybody to be in our club who had a dishonorable record. So I stuck up for him and asked that he be given a chance. In his rough way he appreciated this, and he behaved. Now he is the president of our club. If he'd been kicked out of our gang, I'm afraid he would have gone out and found stormy guys like him and gotten in trouble again.

In our community work we were daily called upon to render various services which normally could be handled without difficulty; but one year we were called on to do the impossible. Fortunately, the Alcoves came to the rescue. A member of an Italian social agency reported a case of a family living in a hotel room on South Clark Street, paying $5 a day. We went to see what could be done. There we met the head of the family, Daniel S., age 37, a short, dark-haired man. Immediately he shook our hand, apologized for the dirty walls and the dilapidated furniture. He introduced us to his wife, Angeline, age 31, sitting on the little iron bed. Her 18-month-old baby, Roseanne, was beside her. Louis, age 5, and Sylvia, age 8, sat on a chair staring at us.

Mrs. S. explained, "It's terrible living here. Been here 40 days, paying $5 a day. The kids can't live normal, can't go to school. We have to eat in restaurants and that costs a lot. Lucky we've been by the Salvation Army. But we can't stay here long. The kids get wild here and nervous too. They like to run around and play in the hall, but the manager and the tenants holler. This is no place for kids, mister. I wish we could find a place. I go out looking for a flat every day but it's no use. Somebody wanted to give us a flat but we had to buy some old chairs, tables, and an icebox for $400. We haven't got that kind of money."

Then Mr. S. spoke up: "We came here about a month ago from New York, where we went about two years ago to visit my folks. In the meantime things began to get tougher. I have chronic tonsillitis and my cheek swells up. I can't work right now, especially with this on my mind. My wife broke her leg last year and it never healed right. She can't lift the baby and take them out to eat by herself. So I have to stay here and help to take care of the kids. While my wife was still in the hospital with a broken leg, Louis got pneumonia. Then the baby got pneumonia. Something is wrong with the baby's legs—she can't walk or stand. Louis's nose keeps bleeding. I can't afford more doctors. I don't know what to do. I'd like to get out of this place, find a small cheap place so I can go to work. I'm handy and I'd paint the place or repair it myself."

We tried to console the family and pledged to help, but inwardly we felt that the search for an apartment of any description would be useless. That same evening I happened to drop in to see the Alcoves, to hang around the club and chew the rag. Since the S. family was on my mind, I related the story to Angelo and the other lads who were around. A few fellows off in the corner stopped playing cards and joined in, asking questions. "Sure," the boys said, "we'll look around and see if we can find a place, but it's going to be tough." Joking at first, Angelo said, "Maybe they could have this place—the club."

"That would be asking too much," I said. "After all, that's asking 25 of your members to make a big sacrifice. But," I emphasized, "if you did do such a thing—well, just imagine how everybody would be proud of you and just think how good it would make you feel."

The boys quietly pondered the proposal. I never saw them in a more serious mood. "So long, fellows," I said, "Got to get going. It's late."

The following evening the boys called a special meeting and unanimously voted to offer their club quarters to the S. family. They contacted me immediately and together with Angelo and Jack, the president, we called on the S. family to tell them about the offer. They were overjoyed. They readily accepted, with warm expressions of gratitude. The following day some of the boys "GI'ed" the floor with scrubbing brushes and mops and later picked up the family with Jack's truck. The Italian Welfare Council, which was the referral agency, was requested to provide a large bed, mattress, sheets, pillowcases, and blankets. And so the S. family was taken out of the hotel and placed where they could move around like human beings. For the children this was better than a home—it was a place to jump and play.

But of course the Alcoves did not expect to be permanent humanitarians. They had a vested interest in becoming apartment hunters. So the 25 members of the club went seeking a flat—myself included. Four days later, John and I, driving by, noticed what might formerly have been a basement flat. We inquired and were told it was not adequate, and besides the building was for sale. We knew the lady who answered our call and explained our situation to her. She told us to try a place a few doors away where a family had recently moved out. We ran to the place and encountered the landlady. She was dubious at first but soon yielded. She called her husband to obtain permission.

We looked over the flat—a spacious five-room apartment, each window adorned with venetian blinds. The rental was $12 a month unheated, and the blinds were only $40. A kitchen stove, icebox, chairs, and table were donated by the landlady. We informed the S. family immediately, and the next day they moved in. What Mr. S. did to this flat a week later would make an interior decorator green with envy.

During World War II most of the social and athletic organizations in our community temporarily disappeared, since they were composed predominantly of young men. However, after the war for about a decade they mushroomed all over our community, and it seemed that they operated with greater zeal and enthusiasm than before. Until about 1955 there were approximately 25 such units with an overall membership of almost 2,000, though during the 1960s their numbers declined, for reasons which will be noted in Chapter 8.

During the 1930s and later, there were also a small number of girls' social clubs, but they never maintained storefront clubrooms. They either met in homes or in one of the social settlement houses or in churches. To some extent, these girls' clubs tried to imitate the young men's clubs, by having jackets or sweaters with the club emblem, holding dances, picnics, and some athletic events.

Our community committee had maintained contacts and working relationships with these groups over the years.

Some of the board of directors and members of our committee have also been members of these clubs, and in turn some of their members have served on our board. In 1946 our committee took the leadership in attempting to coordinate their efforts through an overall organization of delegates or Inter-Club Council, composed of delegates from each club.

Nick Taccio, then the director of our committee, was assigned in the summer of 1946 to contact the 25 clubs then in existence in our area to discuss the plan for the proposed organization. The response was invariably enthusiastic. Each club felt that there was a real need for united effort in club activities, so our committee invited all the representatives to a series of meetings. Twenty-two clubs responded. After a third meeting, the delegates present, with consent of their clubs, decided to form a permanent, independent organization and maintain its headquarters in our committee office. Interestingly enough, other groups, including the two American Legion Posts, a benefit society, and the West Side Community Committee, joined the council.

While our committee is not a social and athletic club, we felt we should participate so that no single organization would dominate the council. As stated in its constitution, this council had as its purpose: "To serve as a clearing house, to assist clubs with their activities, and to encourage and promote social and athletic programs beneficial to all community clubs and local residents."

This Inter-Club Council functioned well as a cooperative venture. For example, from the beginning its purpose was to avoid conflict in dance events and social functions. The council purchased bar supplies and equipment as well as a liquor license so that individual clubs did not have to rent or purchase them each time they sponsored an event.

Another objective of the Inter-Club Council was to discourage certain practices which had the stamp of rackets. While not an extensive practice, occasionally a few enterprising young men would invent the name of a social club and sponsor a dance. Since they attended many dances and had a following, they had little difficulty in selling the tickets. The fake dances usually turned out quite successfully, and the profits were pocketed by the young promoters. The delegates to the Inter-Club Council discussed this issue and urged its members to discourage attendance at such dances. Eventually the practice died out.

Each club paid an annual fee of $15 to be a member of the council and hence to be entitled to these services and equipment. This saved each club money and assured better community support. Besides rendering these services for each club, the Inter-Club Council represented another strong means of action by the people for community improvement and delinquency prevention. For example, all the clubs through their Inter-Club Council in earlier years gave a community-wide Christmas children's party. Approximately $300 was raised each year from voluntary contributions of each club in the council, to which were added donations from local merchants.

Through their participation, the clubs were thus directly and personally exposed to our principles of self-help. Our committee has encouraged such clubs to dig in their own back yard, suggesting that they function as a miniature civic committee in their own block. A number of the clubs have done precisely this.

One year the Buccaneers selected ten youngsters to be sent to our community camp and paid their expenses; the Columbian Knights purchased a movie projector to show outdoor movies to the neighborhood youngsters once a week. Another group sponsored special events for children the year round—parties and games on Christmas, Halloween, and 4th of July. Throughout the summer they showed outdoor movies on a nearby lot, attracting hundreds, young and old. What was probably most significant, this club had a neon sign hanging outside its headquarters with the words "Knights of Roland," a constant reminder to all neighbors that this club was named after and dedicated for Roland Seno, their buddy, a seaman in the U.S. Navy killed in World War II.

While recently discussing the earlier work of these clubs, one of the men said, "The clubs were very important in our lives as young men. We were also interested in doing what we could to help the kids on our street. When we were kids we didn't have a break in life: our parents, coming from the Old Country, didn't know much about what a kid needs here in America. We were pretty much on our own and got into a lot of trouble. But those of us who have been born and raised here, and realize some of the problems, know it's important to see that a kid gets a good education, engages in recreation, and prepares himself for a job. For example, our club used to invite the kids in our neighborhood to use our club for recreational purposes, and we gave parties for the kids and tried to help those who seemed to get into trouble."

These clubs may not solve great problems, but they have been directed toward our fundamental objectives— namely, to encourage our people to concern themselves with the welfare of children and to express this interest by continuous collective action. Through such a spirit the child comes to feel that the community is interested in his well-being and wants him to be a good citizen. And the people themselves learn that our problems are a community responsibility, not only the individual's.

By 1960, with population changes, disruption brought about by the redevelopment housing program, the construction of the University of Illinois, and other changes, many Italian residents were forced to leave the neighborhood. Some social and athletic clubs were not able to perpetuate their organizations, and a few moved out of the area further west. About ten groups remained. Today the number is down to six, and the Inter-Club Council has disbanded. Nevertheless, for a time these clubs were important social groups in our neighborhood, and their activities might be useful to other neighborhoods with similar problems today.

THE CHILDREN'S CAMP

Some of the things we talked about and planned for to improve our community were rather farfetched, castles in the air. But in some cases limited knowledge of what was required to realize our objectives was an advantage rather than a handicap. For example, with thorough information beforehand about what was involved in developing a community camp and picnic grove, we might have been discouraged at the outset. Little did we know at the beginning that the swimming pool which we later constructed at our camp was to cost almost six times the cost of the land! But it seems that Thoreau's admonition applies to our experience: "If you have built castles in the air, your work need not be lost; that is where they should be. Now, put foundations under them."

Early in 1940 our community committee decided to make it possible for many children of our neighborhood to spend time at a summer camp each year. The story of this effort represents a major project our people have promoted, one which excellently illustrates our procedure.

In order to ensure the broadest possible base of participation in this undertaking, we felt we should join forces with our parish church, political leaders, and businessmen. Accordingly, our committee first went to Rev. Remigio Pigato, pastor of Our Lady of Pompeii Church, and suggested that a fund-raising campaign be sponsored jointly by the church and the committee.

The plan was received at first with some skepticism. Rev. Pigato's first reaction was, "You know we are a poor parish. Why, not even the rich parishes here in the city have such things and you expect our poor people, who have a hard time as it is supporting our church, to take on another burden?"

But again our youthful exuberance overcame his argument. We said, "Father, poor as we are, we have the will and the enthusiasm; let us try at any rate to see what we can do." Our padre, it seems, belonged to the you-show-me-first school of thought.

We could show him, for there was already an example in our city of how it could be done. We knew of the efforts of the Russell Square Community Committee, another Chicago Area Project organization, located in the South Chicago steel mills area. Accordingly, we escorted Rev. Pigato to the summer camp near Michigan City, Indiana, which had been built, financed, and managed by the citizens of that area, predominantly Americans of Polish extraction. What we saw at Camp Lange seemed to impress Rev. Pigato.

Shortly after, he readily responded to our plan of sponsoring a community benefit dance to raise funds to purchase land for a camp. This event soon developed into a community-wide undertaking, reaching thousands of persons—residents, businessmen, politicians, and policemen. It was suggested that the chairman of such an event should be a prominent resident of our community, a person whose prestige, influence, and relationships reached into every segment of our population. As it turned out, our alderman's wife, Mrs. William V. Pacelli, was selected as the first chairman of this community benefit dance.

We later discovered this had to be an annual event in order to raise the funds required each year for camp improvements. This first event netted approximately $4,000, with more than 3,000 people sharing, directly or indirectly, in the raising of these funds. In addition, we sponsored benefit dinners with the food donated by local merchants, cooked by neighborhood women, and served by young ladies of our church clubs.

Then came the search for suitable grounds on which to establish our camp. On weekends we would charter a bus, load it up with people, and inspect the various properties that real estate agents referred us to. We examined close to 50 locations before we finally purchased 44 acres of woodland and farmland within an hour's ride of our neighborhood. The property cost $4,000—all we had—and Rev. Pigato seemed to say, "All right, boys, now go to it. Let us see now what amazing things can be done with that dense forest."

Dense forest it was! The property was covered with hickory, poplar, white, black, and burr oaks, elms, and weeping willows, with tangled underbrush, thick wild blackberry bushes, and a liberal sprinkling of poison ivy as close neighbors. How to transform all this into the rest haven we had visualized—and without money!

So we set to work to develop Pompeii Camp, as we called it. With $150 we purchased 9,000 board feet of lumber, salvaged, appropriately enough, from nearby slum dwellings. Some of this lumber we hauled to the woodshop of our local settlement, Hull House, where NYA and WPA workers helped us cut it into appropriate sizes for small cabins, outdoor tables, and sanitation facilities. Then a local grocer made available his truck to haul it to our property.

We publicized the project in every way we could. We announced it through our community newspaper and city press. We talked to church groups, social and athletic clubs, and local businessmen. We got hold of our boys, young men, and older men, and soon put them all to work. We would drive out to our property on weekends with this corps of volunteer workers, first to make clearings, later to erect the first cabins, mess hall, and other buildings.

Included among these volunteers were laborers, clerks, students, three lawyers, an accountant, a local police officer, our truant officer, and others. The spirit of these volunteer workers was especially exemplified by Freddie De Angelo, a short, elderly man with a ruddy complexion and sturdy as an ox, who started to come out to the camp every weekend from the time the work was launched.

Freddie, chief of the digging department, couldn't wait for the rest of the group to drive out with cars, because he was impatient with any delay. Consequently, he got up at five o'clock every Saturday and Sunday to catch the six o'clock train, after which he hiked several miles across the fields to the camp. Sometimes he would come out earlier in the week and camp out, making certain he had among his victuals his loaf of bread and jug of wine. Then he was all set to venture into the quiet of nature amidst the wild flowers, the birds, and the rabbits—free from no trespassing signs.

The chairman of our camping committee was none other than Louis Rovai, another elderly man, a tailor and an active church worker who always got our award of congratulation for surpassing everyone in all our money-raising events. Extremely alert and energetic, Mr. Rovai literally knew everyone in the community and didn't hesitate to approach anyone in support of good works. "For myself I couldn't raise a penny," Mr. Rovai would chuckle, "but as the rich lady I worked for in Evanston used to say: 'For charity, no one should be backward!' "

And indeed Mr. Rovai was not backward when it came to our camp. We should also give him our award for being the most effective propagandist of our camp project: he not only talked about it to the thousands of churchgoers and neighbors, but he would take groups to the camp practi-

cally every weekend to feast on his delicious Italian cooking, which always included an endive salad picked on the
grounds and recommended by Mr. Rovai as being "good
for your blood." While the older Italians preferred *vino* to
water with their meals, Mr. Rovai and others sallied forth
with gusto to drink the cool, sparkling water drawn from
the well.

Other volunteer workers included young men from
our local social and athletic clubs, older delinquent boys,
and young men who had served time in institutions. Some
of these men were on parole, and we would usually have to
clear it with the parole officer before they could be permitted to drive in a car and leave the city. When pictures and
stories of this work appeared in the city newspapers, a great
step was taken in redefining the role of these men and,
most importantly, in giving them a sense of belonging to
a group where no distinctions were made between offenders and law-abiding citizens. Regardless of our backgrounds, we were now all striving to be civic leaders.

Having made a start, we felt heartened by our labors
and mustered the confidence to call on persons outside our
community for additional help. The director of camping
for the Chicago Council, Boy Scouts of America, gladly
offered suggestions on camp layout, organization, and program. The manager of a department of the Chicago Association of Commerce and Industry secured for us, through
the board of education, two small portable school buildings
for $50 each, which when put together became an excellent
mess hall, 20 X 60 feet. The Chicago Community Trust
gave us a grant of $1,000 for equipment and operating
expenses for the first year. Later we became a participating
agency in the Community Fund, and part of the camp expenses were met through this source. In addition, various
members of the staff of the Chicago Area Project helped us
in innumerable ways in planning and promoting this
project.

Amateur carpenters one and all, the erection of the mess hall building was for us an Herculean feat. To begin with, this building had first to be dismantled in Chicago, where it was serving as a schoolroom adjacent to a high school. In this task we were fortunate in having the aid of some of the men who volunteered in the construction of the Russell Square Community Committee's camp.

After many months of sweat (sometimes blood and tears, too), this huge structure was completed. Gradually we equipped it and furnished the cabins. Outdoor cooking facilities were constructed by one of our campers who wanted to use up excess energy. A tile contractor picked as his project the construction of a fireplace in our mess hall, decorating it artistically with tile pieces in an array of colors. An old milk wagon, bought for $7, lost its wheels and became a toolhouse. Used doubledecker steel beds were bought for 75¢ each, and for mattresses we used straw ticks which were made and donated by two mothers of our neighborhood.

An old varnished tank, purchased for $25 and hoisted on top of four telephone poles, became our water tower, and water was pumped into it with an old gasoline engine we purchased from a local farmer for a few dollars. We also constructed showers and recreational facilities. A small farmhouse was erected with the aid of a local farmer, who was engaged as our caretaker. Later he was replaced by one of the young men of our neighborhood, who also functioned as our camp director while his wife did the cooking for the children.

Not the least of our improvements was our religious grotto, which served as our outdoor church. Built of cement blocks as a sort of semicircular structure, this building required engineering knowledge before our "tile man" could complete the job. The steel—and the knowledge— were supplied by the Chicago Bridge and Iron Works. A statue of the Madonna, flanked by two angels and other religious objects, were donated by persons in our community. A huge, 30-foot cross was placed opposite the grotto.

In the early years of our camp operation, we had to drive the children to the nearby forest preserves for swimming since our property lacked such facilities, an arrangement which was inconvenient and unsatisfactory. Early in the history of this project we planned, therefore, for the eventual construction of a swimming pool on our property.

In 1944 we again started to sponsor an annual community benefit dance, reserving the proceeds for our swimming pool fund. Again, in our limited knowledge we thought at first that a few thousand dollars would be sufficient. We consulted our advisory committee—a group composed of interested businessmen who offered our community committee advice and other assistance as needs arose—and other technical consultants; it was estimated that the pool would cost approximately $10,000. Of course this was quite a jolt, but there was no retreating.

Our benefit affairs continued to be as successful as the first ones, each event netting approximately $3,000. But each year inflation kept skyrocketing the costs. Completed in 1945, the swimming pool cost $20,000, and the additional bathing and sanitation facilities cost us another $5,000.

This pool greatly enhanced the value of the property and enriched the content of our camping program. In addition it served, as we had earlier contemplated, as a real country club and picnic grove available to every person in our neighborhood. Due to its proximity to the city, plus the fact that it could be reached by means of suburban trains, these facilities were available the year round for outings, picnics, and weekend trips.

The program activities at the camp were planned and operated entirely by local leaders—older brothers, fathers, and uncles of the boys who attended camp. The point to be emphasized, however, is that this was something more than just a camp. It was our camp, crude and rustic as it was. The money was raised in our community. The work was done by the people of our community, and the camp was managed and directed by our own people. It was a place that our people owned, where they could send their children and go themselves, free from the feeling that they were being given charity or called underprivileged.

The idea of a camp served dramatically as a device to enlist the interest, the help, and the financial assistance of thousands of people in our community. It served as an excellent medium to arouse concern over neighborhood problems. Even more important is the way it served to develop a tradition for this type of work—a tradition in sharp contrast with the delinquent and criminal activities that had long been the reputation of our area.

Our committee operated Pompeii Camp for about 15 years. But as the community began to change, new problems and new issues arose. By 1955 we were gravely concerned about the future of the Near West Side. The new expressways to the north and east, the projected plans for urban renewal and redevelopment of the area, together with decline in the population—these changes were creating uncertainties and affecting the morale of the community. In the face of these more pressing problems, our leaders lost much of their earlier enthusiasm for camping.

When we heard that the Near Northwest Civic Committee, another group affiliated with the Chicago Area Project, was very much interested in sending children to a summer camp, arrangements were made to lease the property to them. The Near Northwest Civic Committee, located about a mile north of our area, was the logical group to take over the camp. It had a history similar to ours, identical philosophy and goals, and indeed it operated in a more stable area than ours and had a very strong organization with enthusiastic leaders, broad participation of local residents in its youth welfare program, and adequate sources of financial support.

Since the early 1960s, under the leadership of the Near Northwest Civic Committee, under the leadership of Dan "Moose" Brindisi, Pompeii Camp has been greatly improved. The old buildings have been renovated, electricity installed, and new cabins and recreational facilities built. As a result, many more children are attending it each summer and on weekends the year round.

Chapter 6

OPENING
LEGITIMATE OPPORTUNITIES

WORKING WITH DELINQUENTS

The clinic, the court, the reformatory, and probation and parole services are essential in relation to the task of treatment and rehabilitation of adolescents who have already been labeled delinquent, but they alone cannot obtain the desired results, as various studies have shown. Follow-up studies based on official records even today show that two-thirds to three-fourths of the delinquents dealt with by correctional agencies continue in delinquency and crime despite treatment and rehabilitation efforts. Institutions, by their very nature, cannot "correct."

Correct what? This assumes that the offender is sick, when actually the community or society is sick and should be regarded as the patient. We have given unrealistic if not impossible tasks to custodial institutions, and in the process we have fooled the public and placed heavy burdens and frustrations on institutional personnel.

We knew from our experience that representatives from these official agencies were frequently hindered in their attempts to help children and young people with problems, partly because of what they symbolized. They were outside the pale, far removed and regarded with suspicion, if not downright enmity. In many cases, children or their parents would not open up in the presence of these agents and at best would merely give lip service to their suggestions or requests.

We must confess that our community was itself remiss in not tackling this problem earlier. We sat back for many years watching the police, social workers, and other well-meaning people trying to help our youngsters, while we ourselves reacted with indifference and lack of concern. Perhaps that is the history of all immigrant groups during their coming of age. Finally we realized we had to join forces with law enforcement officials, social workers, educators, and administrators, and share with them responsibility for helping our young people.

We went to our schools, to the juvenile police officers in our district, to the juvenile court authorities, and to our officials at the State Training School for Boys at St. Charles, and we expressed our interest and willingness to establish contact with each offender from our community coming to their attention. Without exception, all these officials through the years have been eager to accept our cooperation.

This meant first of all that members of our committee, staff members, and other community residents had to be in frequent contact with the juvenile authorities. We were in and out of the police station regularly, meeting with the juvenile police officer to talk over problems of children who were in trouble or to discuss community conditions related to these problems. Frequently the juvenile police officer would come to us directly; he would meet with youngsters at our neighborhood centers and talk to parents and other adult groups, urging them to assume responsibility for meeting the needs of the youngsters who engaged in delinquent activities.

Since some of our members had themselves been in trouble with the law, processed and labeled delinquent, we had some insights into why children became delinquent and how the juvenile justice system operates. Moreover, we knew the people, their family structure, culture, and community resources. We felt that this background would give us certain advantages in attempting to reach those youngsters who were being handled by the police, courts, and correctional institutions and intervene on their behalf.

Our plan was to enlist local young men as volunteers to encourage and advise those boys who were getting in trouble and assist them by giving them constructive opportunities, though some people, such as caseworkers at local agencies, were taken aback by our plan and seriously questioned the ability of these volunteers.

Ernest Shaeffer, our local juvenile officer at the Maxwell station, welcomed our assistance and was eager to refer "cases." I would usually contact him every week, or he would visit our center to discuss boys who needed help. In some instances we already had information on such boys through our many neighborhood contacts. Our staff would then enlist the assistance of volunteers who expressed an interest in working with these boys, aided, of course, by our staff, who provided back-up services as needed.

We also found several probation officers at the juvenile court who were pleased to have our help. One of these was the late Max West. To my knowledge he did not have any academic degrees, but he was an earthy philosopher with a delightful sense of humor, deep understanding, and folk wisdom. He also had common sense and a glowing spirit which enabled him to establish rapport with even the most intransigent. With all these qualities he probably didn't need our help, but he knew you have to use all the help you can get on those mean streets.

There were others, like Edward Nerad at the juvenile court, who welcomed our help. I believe our efforts and those of the other community committees affiliated with the Chicago Area Project demonstrated that volunteers could contribute to the treatment of delinquents. For example, the Juvenile Court of Cook County today has a special program to recruit and train volunteers to assist probation officers with their cases. In addition, the new Juvenile Court Act provides for the use of court designees by the judges; in lieu of either official probation or commitment, a delinquent may be turned over for supervision and counseling to a private citizen on a voluntary basis.

To illustrate further our work with officially designated delinquents, let us take from our files the story of one of these boys. We'll call him Jim. When he was 17 years old, Jim was involved in petty stealing, jackrolling, burglarizing, and purchasing as well as selling stolen articles. When apprehended for one of these offenses he was ushered into the juvenile court, with his brother and a representative of our committee appearing on his behalf. In view of his past truancy, school difficulties, and unfavorable record at Montefiore Special School, it seemed likely that he would be committed to the Illinois State Training School for Boys. However, because our committee offered to furnish wholesome contacts and employment suited to his skills, the judge agreed to release him to us for supervision.

We got Jim a job with a local merchant who was a member of our committee. In this small manufacturing establishment, the relationships were informal, warm, and personal. Since it had been apparent to us from Jim's previous employment record that he could not adjust to formal, rigid regulations in a large factory, the type of job we secured for him was a necessary and essential factor in his rehabilitation.

In addition, Jim had almost daily contacts with various members of our committee. The result was that Jim participated regularly in the committee's social and club activities and later volunteered his services in the construction of our summer camp.

At the beginning Jim did get into some difficulties at work. He was frequently late, unreliable, and shiftless. When he didn't feel like working he would quit for a while and return at his convenience. Sometimes he would "quit" before he was to be fired. This went on for several years. In the interim we had placed him in other small businesses operated by two of our members. Here, too, he had only modest success. Several years later, however, he returned to the first job, where he continued for several years until his employer moved his business to another state. Later he moved on to other jobs.

We worked with Jim over 20 years ago. Over these years he has kept out of trouble and is now a useful citizen. Had Jim been committed to the training school—where 20 years ago his incarceration would have cost $3,000 (today the cost in Illinois is over $20,000 per year)—he might have learned to be a criminal.

Another illustration of the way a delinquent's life can be improved is in this autobiographical document:

Shortly after finishing grammar school, I started the most exciting time of my life. I began to get into the rackets. I knew a lot of people who had gone into the bootlegging racket, manufacturing and selling alky. There was money in it. One man was worth a quarter of a million dollars. I worked for him. At first I did many odd jobs; I would drive his car, make deliveries, carry messages, and even handle large sums of money. This brought me into contact with persons in the racket. I was picked up many times but was never convicted.

During those years, money was like water, and the struggle to get it was fierce and ruthless. Fights, hijacking, extortions, one-way rides, cold and bloody murder were all part of the day's work. As I grew older, I became part of these things.

With the end of Prohibition, things began to change. With all the contacts and friends I had in the booze racket, new doors of opportunity opened for me. For about two years I worked for a big shot in the muscle racket. My job was to muscle "payments" from grocers, butchers, and other small businessmen. I had some narrow escapes in this racket, and my job ended when some of the big shots I worked for were bumped off.

When the Depression came along, jobs were scarce. I had to get along by odd jobs. A few breaks here and a few breaks there, and the days went by. Some, like me, managed to stay out of trouble. I drifted along for a while and then heard of the WPA. Besides, I had a family to support and needed a steady income.

Of all things, I was assigned to do recreation work with children in my neighborhood! This was strange to me. A lot of people in the neighborhood were responsible for the work. I worked with them, got acquainted with them, and began to do the duties assigned to me. Gradually, my viewpoint began to change. The people I worked with kept after me. I began to get interested in the work. The change was slow, but as I got acquainted more with the people interested in the work, I could see that a fellow might be a big shot in a different way, and without risking his life to do it.

I kept on in this work, helping to organize kids' programs, and finally got a full-time job. Of all things, I am happy in it and hope that I can continue for many more years.

It has been more than eight years since I was in the rackets. Looking back now, this past seems like a dream, almost unbelievable. I could not go back to the rackets because I couldn't let my new friends down. I would not disappoint them.

After a few years with the WPA, the federally funded project terminated, and the young man who wrote the above was employed by the Chicago Area Project as a community organizer. In a short time he qualified for the state's civil service examination, became a delinquency prevention coordinator, and was given responsibilities to plan, promote, and develop community programs similar to ours in other parts of the city. This indigenous leader was considered very resourceful, not only by the local residents but by the agencies as well. How he dealt with a difficult situation involving the theft of 200 chairs from a local settlement house is described in the following account:

> Usually every morning I went to the coffee shop of the settlement house to have coffee with Mr. Burt, the program director. We often talked about many important problems and issues at these "coffee and" sessions. But I didn't expect what took place on this particular morning. As Mr. Burt and I were sitting down, in walks Miss D., the head resident, and one of her workers, puffing excitedly on their cigarettes.
>
> "Our chairs—our 200 chairs from the auditorium—they disappeared—stolen over the weekend. We reported the incident to the police, but we have not been notified of any progress."
>
> Well, I just sat there and grinned as Mr. Burt and the lady social workers looked troubled.
>
> Finally, all eyes were directed to me and pointing they said, "You've got to help us. Somebody in this community stole those folding chairs."
>
> "OK," I said, "But I have to do it my way. Mr. Burt," I said, "come with me."
>
> We got in my jalopy and stopped at one of the social and athletic clubs. I thought it was all right to have Mr. Burt with me because he was becoming accepted by our community. In the clubhouse I started to make small talk with some of the guys and at the same time looked over the type of chairs. I could quickly spot the settlement house chairs, but to make sure, I playfully turned one upside down to see if the agency's name was stenciled on the bottom. Well, we did this with about six clubhouses, and by this time I became convinced that the job was not pulled by any of the guys from our social and athletic clubs.
>
> Who else in our community would want 200 chairs? How about the undertakers? When I told Mr. Burt we were visiting our funeral parlors, he thought I was whacky. We visited five of these establishments, but there was no evidence of the settlement house chairs.

Who else would want 200 chairs? Who else but the bookie joints, I speculated. When I announced this to Mr. Burt, he thought I'd definitely gone off my rocker. We drove to a well-known bookie joint on South Halsted Street; this time I told Mr. Burt to wait outside in the car. As I'd told him, I had to do this my way. I walked in the joint, and sure enough the first chair I picked up had the name of the settlement house clearly stenciled on the bottom. I went up to the head man.

"Hi, Mr. Frank." I said, "I'm Charlie, the son of Alberto."

Big Frank smiled, "Sure, sure, I remember. What can I do for you, Charlie?"

"Mr. Frank, Those chairs in this joint, I think they spell trouble. You know, they belong to the settlement house, and if the newspaper heard about this, they could make a big stink about it."

"My young man," Big Frank said, "I think you worry too much. Here, have a couple of cigars and relax. Besides, we only have a few chairs here. The rest of them are at other joints. But if you want to check this out, go see the big boss in Cicero."

I thanked Mr. Frank and went out in the car where Mr. Burt was waiting. "Let's go," I said, "We're now going to Cicero."

Mr. Burt was perplexed, to put it mildly. We finally got to a certain nightclub in Cicero, and after I was checked out by the doorman I was admitted to see the big man. I told him my story, that I worked for the settlement house now, that in a sense I was on the spot, and that returning the chairs would make me look good and avoid possible trouble for them. The big man listened but said little.

Finally, he said, "Go to City Hall in Chicago and see Mr. Dickson, the alderman's secretary. I'll call him. He'll take care of things. The chairs will be returned."

When I got back to the car and told Mr. Burt we were going to City Hall, he was absolutely beside himself. As directed, I went to see Mr. Dickson and gave him the details. My mission was over. Now we would have to wait.

Several days later at our usual "coffee and" session, two big Irish cops walked in and asked for me. "The chairs—

they're in the paddy wagon. Where do you want them delivered?"

As I gave them instructions to put them back in the auditorium, the head resident, puffing furiously on her cigarette, spoke up: "Where did you find those chairs?" she said sternly.

"Lady," the cop said, "we found them in an empty lot."

A Community Responsibility

Our committee takes the position that the offender is a product of the influences of his family and community. It is therefore the community's responsibility to welcome him back to the neighborhood upon his release from an institution and try to incorporate him into the conventional life of the community.

Unfortunately, we have not succeeded in keeping all our youngsters out of institutions. Some boys persist in delinquent conduct despite all our efforts, But even when our efforts fail we do not abandon the offender; we continue to show our concern for his welfare by keeping in touch with him while he is in the institution. We visit him personally, send him a copy of our community newspaper, write him letters, give him a little money to purchase candy, cigarettes, or personal items, and in other ways try to keep up his spirit and morale and give him the feeling that some of his neighbors have not forgotten him. These personal contacts enable us to keep up a continuing relationship so that when he is released we can work with him, his family, the parole agency, and other persons who are interested in his welfare.

The willingness of our people to share the responsibility for the reformation of our delinquents quite frequently gives the juvenile police officer, judge, or parole agent an alternative to commitment to an institution. We can be the link between our neighborhood resources and the law enforcement agencies; we can mobilize the aid of our local leaders, young men of our social and athletic clubs, parents, priests, teachers, and local social workers in efforts to rehabilitate delinquents and older offenders.

The procedure which I have discussed in working with delinquents is often referred to today as "diversion," which means that alleged delinquents, particularly those who have committed noncriminal or status offenses, are referred to community resources. Today, getting the community involved in various treatment strategies is the name of the game in the juvenile justice system. It is heartening to see experts in this field proposing that ordinary citizens be allowed to play a meaningful role in helping delinquents become reintegrated in the community. There is now at last a recognition of the value of volunteers, businessmen, ex-offenders, and youths who have never been in trouble to serve as advocates for youths in trouble. We are beginning to learn, as the Chicago Area Project proposed a long time ago, that "citizens and volunteers may be more competent in achieving the desirable goal of the '70s—reintegration of juvenile offenders into the community—than the professionals."[44]

In Illinois, for example, the number of juveniles in correctional institutions has declined from over two thousand to less than one thousand. This reduction has taken place partly because the juvenile court is committing fewer children to the state's institutions. The court is making greater use of probation and using more highly trained probation officers with smaller caseloads. It is also welcoming volunteer probation officers and seeking out community resources. The State Department of Corrections, in turn, is turning to community-based programs. These include more paroles, furloughs, authorized absences from the institutions, group homes, and foster homes.

Perhaps the most innovative approach, regarded by some as radical, was undertaken a few years ago by Dr. Jerome Miller, then head of Massachusetts's Youth Division. (From 1972 to 1974, Miller was director of the Illinois Department of Children and Family Services.) Miller closed down almost all the Massachusetts juvenile correctional institutions: juveniles committed to the state by the courts were simply placed in community-based facilities. These included a variety of privately run facilities, the state paying the cost. The only institution for juveniles which remained was a small facility for less than one hundred children who were considered security risks and required institutional care.

In recent years only a few neighborhood Italian boys have been in the Illinois Training School. In 1940, when we started the practice of systematically visiting our boys in this institution, there were about ten boys from our neighborhood. We believe our efforts in reaching boys early in their delinquency and preventing them from being labeled delinquents have had an effect.

Undoubtedly there have also been many other influences and social changes in the lives of our people to account for the downward trend in the rates of delinquency in our community. For example, the Italian people during the past two decades have been making substantial gains in the social, economic, and political life of the city and state. Children nowadays are growing up in an improved social situation as compared with their parents and older brothers and sisters, who lived in an immigrant society characterized by cultural and generational conflicts, low social status, and limited opportunities. The period of our community enterprise's existence has coincided with this advance made by the Italian people of our area, so it is difficult to prove it; but it is our firm conviction that our enterprise can be counted as one of the forces responsible for reducing delinquency.

EMPLOYING ADULT EX-OFFENDERS

Finding jobs for adult ex-offenders was especially difficult in the early days of our work. Some of our local businessmen occasionally provided jobs for men coming out of prison—but not many. Since a condition for parole was that an inmate have a job waiting for him, local merchants would often pledge a job and sign the necessary papers, but more often than not this was just a set-up—a plan to fool the system, though sometimes it did succeed. A family would go, say, to a local contractor and ask the owner to sign the necessary application stating that upon release he would hire an inmate as a plumber, painter, or truck driver, even though when the man came out of prison there was no job, or at best it would last only a few weeks until a steady job could be found.

So we were often called upon by families or the men themselves to find jobs. We went to our local industries and often, on an individual basis, we had some success. Other people turned us down, explaining that in their business employees had to be bonded and insurance companies would not bond ex-convicts.

Sometimes the men would tell us of their trials and tribulations as they tried to find work. Some men would be honest and tell the employer they had been in prison; more often than not, they would be refused consideration. Some men lied on their applications forms, denying any criminal record and covering their prison years with a false work history; in most instances they were eventually discovered and then fired for lying. It was a vicious circle, and even today it is a noose around the ex-offender's neck.

Even the state government had a policy of not hiring ex-offenders. Then in the early 1940s Shaw challenged the state on this issue, establishing a precedent that later enabled our committee to recommend young men for community work. I remember vividly the time when Shaw intervened on behalf of Sydney, a 39-year-old man who had just been discharged (in this case without parole, since he had served his full sentence, 20 years) from Stateville, Illinois's maximum security prison, a medieval fortress in Joliet. Before that he had spent another 10 years in various juvenile institutions, or a total of 30 years out of his 39 years in custody as a ward of the state.

I met Sydney the day he came to the Institute for Juvenile Research. He had no other place to go. His parents had died while he was in prison, and an only brother had broken all ties with him. He was ill at ease, nervous, and distraught. There was no smile on his face or cheer in his voice. He was in no shape to be applying for help in some impersonal agency. But he came to see Shaw, whom he had known for 20 years and for whose research he had written his life history.[45]

Shaw and I talked with Sidney and asked him if he had any plans. Naturally, he said his first objective was to find a place to live. We made suggestions for lodgings and then discussed the question of employment. He said he could contact some friends whom he had met in prison and who had assured him of help, but he was fearful that this would obligate him to the criminal world. He said he would do this only as a last resort.

Shaw then asked Sydney how he would like to work at the institute, if arrangements could be made. Sydney was stunned, for the idea was not only incongruous but unprecedented. Moreover, he was reluctant to accept; he did not want something contrived. He was assured that it would be a meaningful job and that he could make a contribution to our work. Slowly he warmed up to the idea, and Shaw and I marched up to the superintendent's office. The superintendent was even more stunned than Sydney. He got up from his chair and, pointing a stern finger at Shaw, bellowed, "Do you realize what you are requesting? Even if we could get approval in Springfield [the state capital], can you imagine the risks? Why, if the newspapers found out that we hired an ex-convict it would make the front page."

After the superintendent cooled down, Shaw continued to set forth his proposal in his inimitable way. In essence he said: here is a human being who has been severely deprived, who has suffered and has been cast out of society for decades. The state has spent thousands of dollars for his custody. It now turns him loose and expects society to employ this emotionally handicapped person. If the great State of Illinois is not now willing to provide a legitimate opportunity for this human being, why should it expect people in the conventional world to give him a chance? Shaw always spoke with genuine concern and empathy for the offender, and after this eloquent argument, I think the superintendent began to admire him and to feel a bit ashamed. "If you're willing to stick your neck out, I guess we should support you."

Shortly after that Sydney was hired, and for years he performed useful work, at first copying records and gradually moving on to statistical work on various research projects. Eventually he was married, and he worked continuously at the institute until he passed away a few years ago at age 63.

Thereafter it became easier to employ ex-offenders in state service. Encouraged by this precedent, our committee recommended a young man from our community, a man who had served five years in the reformatory, for a position as a community worker. This person was an effective leader who remained in charge of one of our neighborhood centers for about five years. Later he secured employment in private business, married, purchased his own home, and continued as a member of the board of directors of our committee.

In later years we were able to recommend many others for employment with the state. Some of these persons used state employment to get started in the legitimate world and later moved into other occupations. Others continued their education and stayed in the field. Two such young men, an Italian and a black, both earned their master's degrees in sociology and social work and are professionally occupied.

While many ex-offenders still encounter difficulties in securing employment, the situation is greatly improved. Many projects have been launched in recent years especially designed to secure jobs for ex-offenders. Some agencies, including our own, have begun to employ such persons as paraprofessionals and as professionals in programs for the rehabilitation of offenders. Many industries have opened up their doors and are more liberal in their hiring practices. While problems still exist, there has unquestionably been progress.

Although employment is crucial in helping the offender make the transition from prison to the outside world, other elements are necessary to his rehabilitation, too. Perhaps even more important is the way the family receives him—whether they are accepting or rejecting.

We were on the whole always fortunate in working with the families of Italian offenders. Rarely did an Italian family reject a son or a husband when he went to prison. While he was incarcerated, the family would visit him regularly and try to pull all kinds of strings to hasten his parole. When he returned to the community there was rejoicing, family gatherings, and of course lavish dinners and parties. We learned from workers in other areas that these practices were often in sharp contrast with those of some other ethnic and racial groups, who sometimes rejected and abandoned the offender.[46] As a result such persons might become demoralized, resort to drink, and continue in their criminal activities.

Another ingredient necessary for rehabilitation which we found operating in our work with offenders was the role of the peer groups and friends in the conventional world.

Here again the offender's companions or friends welcomed the men who returned from institutions and provided opportunities for social activities. Finally, the social climate of the community is important in redirecting delinquents or older offenders. If the residents are indifferent or hostile toward them, they will readily sense it. Of course our organization's programs have been helpful in changing these attitudes.

As for our failures, this is our guiding rule: Never give up with the offender. One never knows when there will be a turning point. During periods of outward failure, subtle influences may be at work in ways we cannot understand at the time. Some former delinquents and adult ex-offenders who eventually became productive citizens have come to me and expressed their appreciation for how they felt we helped them.

JOHN ROMANO

The backbone of our organization was and is the volunteer, that man or woman who becomes enthusiastic about helping other human beings. We've had many such people; one was the late John Romano, who, in the following story written in 1955, describes how he became an active volunteer, officer, and later chairman of our adult parole committee.

> My first contact with the West Side Community Committee goes back to the early 1940s. I knew then about its work from Sam Serpe, who lived across the street from me, Paul D'Arco, and Emil Peluso. At the time, the committee operated a neighborhood center on my block, so I knew they were trying to help kids and promote programs for community betterment. Since I knew so many of the fellows in the committee, I naturally drifted into it and became a member.

We used to have meetings regularly on Friday nights where many things were discussed: how to help delinquent kids, tournaments, camping, visits to institutions to see young men and adults in prison, how to cooperate with the schools, public parks, and social agencies. Also frequently discussed was how to interest other people in the community in our program and of course how to raise funds.

After the meetings we usually went out for coffee or pizza or beer, sometimes bowling, and we continued our discussion. It was always in conjunction with the community problems and the programs we wanted to promote. Sometimes it seemed we accomplished more in these informal social gatherings than at the meetings. But I guess both were necessary.

I started to become more active about 1950. Paul D'Arco was always at our house, since at that time he was courting my sister, and he always explained things so well. Paul was a college graduate and had real ability, and he could be very convincing; so I became more involved. Also at this time some of us got married, and we began to bring in our wives and other women as members.

I remember one night at my house we got into a long discussion about fellows from our neighborhood who were in prison, and Paul explained that Nick Taccio, our new worker who succeeded Tony Sorrentino, wanted to make special efforts to help these fellows. He explained a plan whereby some of us would visit the men in prison, appear before the parole board on their behalf and then work in every way possible to help them get reestablished when they came out. I also learned about this program from another friend, Ross "Weegie" Bruno, and it began to sound to me like the sort of things I really wanted to get involved in.

We began to make arrangements with the prison staff to meet the men in the institution on a social basis. It was strictly informal. Sometimes we would meet in the warden's office with four or five fellows, but when needed we also met with the fellow individually. We did this especially when a parole hearing was coming up. We would talk with the fellow about his problems, employment, family, home conditions, and stuff like that. We would try to make it as friendly as possible, and at times even throw in a little humor. In other words, we were building up a relationship, putting them at ease, and showing them that we were friends and neighbors on the outside who were trying to help them.

I think these visits also helped build up their morale while they were in the institution. I remember one incident when Mike brought to my attention a guard who for some reason used to pick on him. But after our visits, which were noted by the guard, he apparently began to ease off on Mike and in general seemed to cooperate.

On one trip we went to Pontiac Reformatory with our advisory committee, made up of businessmen. We were escorted through the shops and corridors where we met some of the fellows we knew. We asked the guards if we could say hello and exchange some greetings with the fellows. Well, they permitted us to do this, and it brought a little cheer into the drab place. We met some of the fellows three or four times during the tour, and each time we would stop, say hello, and carry on a brief conversation. Some of these fellows we ran into wore red caps, which means they were trusties, freer to move around than the other prisoners. Well, such visits, tours, and informal conversations seemed to have a terrific effect on their morale.

When we visited the fellows we would talk about everything in general—the baseball games, the fights on TV, about the activities in prison, their outlook on things in general. The fellows were very open and cooperative and told us of their problems with prison life, and they asked us a lot of questions about the outside, about their families, friends, and about the activities of the committee.

Our committee's visits were considered in a special category by the prison officials; that is, they were not counted as official visits, which were limited. Our social visits were extra—a bonus so to speak.

Besides building a relationship with the inmates in the prison, we also got very friendly with the assistant warden and the chaplain. We sometimes had lunch with them and some of the guards, and once with one of the parole officers. These staff persons seemed to be impressed with what we were doing and saw real value in our program. On one occasion they asked us if we could help other men outside our community who were eligible for parole and who needed employment and the kind of support we were giving. We explained that we could not go out of our area because of limited personnel; also we were effective because we were working with men with our background and from our own community. However, we did refer the parole officer to the Chicago Federation of Community Committees; as a result I believe that help was secured for other men through other committees similar to our own.

Another interesting thing is that other inmates heard about our program, our committee became rather well known, and a lot of other fellows would contact us and make a plea for help. We sometimes could make exceptions if the man lived near our community, but it was impossible to cover the whole city. We would not be able to do an effective job if we branched out too far. Here again we would try to refer these men to other committees, but such groups did not exist in every community. The answer was really to organize a committee like ours in every neighborhood, as Shaw often suggested. I hope that some day people get together in neighborhoods all over this city and try to tackle this problem—not all the problems of the country, but just those little but important problems of the type we were working on.

If one of our parolees moved out of our community, we would not drop him because of a boundary problem or anything like that. After all, after we had built up a relationship we would continue with it even if the man moved away to an entirely different area.

When the men come out of prison we invite them to our meetings and social functions. But in addition we try to get one of our members to relate on an even more personal basis with each of the parolees. We have found that each member of our subcommittee on parole has a little more specific interest in certain fellows; and he tends to get a little closer to them and keep up a relationship that is more meaningful. In this way we have found that they can handle situations more effectively.

For instance, I meet with Mike often on the street, at the committee, at social gatherings, or wherever it may be. Recently he told me he was unhappy with his job—not enough pay. He was interested in earning extra money. I looked into this and I was able to get him a part-time job on weekends. Now that's keeping him very happy. And that is the way it goes; whatever problems each of the fellows have, they confide in one member of the committee in a rather casual and informal manner. Sometimes the fellows talk about their problems without even knowing it, and that's the way it works.

Even our trips to the prison are arranged informally. A staff member plans the details and I may get a phone call to find out if I'm available. The other members of our committee who are interested are also called, and that's how we get going.

Parole hearings are very important. We are always well received, and the parole board members usually comment to the family that they are familiar with our work, that we have been to the prison on many visits, and that they are happy to see that the family and our committee are both interested and working in the interest of the particular inmate to assist him in his rehabilitation.

We have also built up good relationships with the parole officer. We have met with the superintendent of this agency and his staff to make known our interest in parolees and to ensure them of our willingness to cooperate with the parole agent. This is very important, because it helps us to deal with the fears and anxieties that parolees have toward their agents. When the fellows come out of prison they are apprehensive—they think, well, if a parole agent is coming, he's going to try to send them back to prison and things of that sort.

We try to build a relationship with the parole agent and parolee; we try to give them a friendlier feeling toward each other. We have met with several parole agents, and they have been very cooperative. We make clear that we don't want to take away any of the authority of the parole agent or to have them feel we're trying to tell them what to do. So you see, it's one big circle; we try to establish friendly relations between the officers and the men out on parole.

When the fellows come out of prison, they usually drop in at our office and neighborhood center. We invite them to our meetings and to our social activities or to just drop in for a visit. Some of the fellows have become members; others have not. There's no pressure exerted. Some of the fellows have volunteered some nights when we sponsor a carnival to raise money jointly with Our Lady of Pompeii Church. Others have helped out at the CYO Center, or getting ads for our dance program book, helping at the camp or just doing odd jobs for us at our office—anything they want to do that gets them interested and makes them feel that they are a part of the West Side Community Committee. We try to convey to them that we are not just an organization to belong to; they are part and parcel of it.

To summarize our parole programs I might point out that we have developed the following procedures: (1) initial contact with parolee's family; (2) visits to the institution; (3) corresponding with the offender in the institution; (4) representing the offender at parole hearings with the family; (5) assisting in securing employment (before or after parole); (6) contact with the offender immediately after release from the institution; (7) assisting the offender in getting things cleared up; and (8) involving the parolee in the committee program and gaining status in the community.

What have we accomplished? Have we been successful? How about our failures? Well, I can't give a scientific explanation but I can tell what happened.

From 1947 to 1955 we worked with 34 men on parole. Two of the men moved away from our neighborhood and were not active. Both of these later had parole violations and were returned to institutions. However, we still continued to visit them in the institution, and one later became re-established and finally stayed out of crime. Two men never active with the committee were killed in the course of committing new crimes. Of the remaining 30 men who were active with us, two were returned on new indictments. Even if we say we failed with six men, this comes to about a 17 percent failure rate—or about 6 percent failure with those actively involved. I believe this is a much better record than normally is achieved by the traditional procedures.

I have been vitally interested in this work, actually fascinated by it. I guess because of my work in this field. I was elected for two terms as president of the West Side Community Committee.

Chapter 7

THE HARD TO REACH
YOUTH PROJECT

INDIGENOUS WORKERS

Our work with street corner groups in the early 1930s and '40s was frowned upon by social agencies. Groupwork outside an agency setting was considered unorthodox. The notion of using leaders who were indigenous to the community was even worse; they were at first referred to as "untrained," a charge often made against workers employed in programs sponsored by the Chicago Area Project.

But in the early 1950s many social agencies began very seriously to question the adequacy of services for youth. The continued rise in juvenile delinquency seemed to suggest that the methods then being followed by those conventional social agencies were not effective. Citizens were asking more questions and demanding better services.

In 1955 the Welfare Council of Metropolitan Chicago established a Youth Services Committee which studied this problem and raised two basic questions: (1) Can our present agencies effectively serve the youth in our city who are not now being served? (2) Do we need new agencies or new settings in which to serve our youth? The committee developed a community plan for youth services, established criteria for developing a program and urged social agencies to broaden the scope of their work to include more reaching-out measures and aggressive groupwork techniques that would give more help, guidance, and support to adolescents, especially those in the inner city areas.

This formulation of the problem soon led to the launching of the Hard to Reach Youth Project, spurred by special funding from the Community Fund of Chicago. Dozens of agencies embarked on street work with corner groups or gangs of adolescents by making use of "detached workers"; that is, young workers who carried on groupwork essentially outside the traditional agency settings.

As described in the two previous chapters, the West Side Community Committee had pioneered in this approach, now being introduced as a new venture. However, we applied for participation in the Hard to Reach Youth Project and were readily accepted by the Welfare Council and Community Fund. In our design for this project we included, of course, the use of indigenous leaders on a part-time basis.

At the time this program was in operation, I was no longer the staff worker assigned to the West Side Community Committee. By 1946 I had been given administrative responsibilities in the Chicago Area Project, but I continued to maintain close contact with the work of the committee, both as a member of the board of directors and as a district supervisor of the state staff. My successors were Nick Taccio and Emil Peluso, who served as executive director and program worker, respectively, for the committee. Both were highly qualified; they were college graduates, residents of the community, and members of our organization for many years.

Among the indigenous workers employed by the committee in connection with the Hard to Reach Youth Project were John Giampa and Frank Gabitz, whose work is described in two staff reports which comprise this chapter. Joseph Gitlin, a university student, assisted with some of the recording and report writing. In addition, two psychiatrists from the Institute for Juvenile Research, Dr. George Klumpner and Dr. Bernard Lifson, provided psychiatric consultation to the workers.

Changes started to take place after World War II in one section of the Near West Side in the area inhabited by the Kings and Knights, two gangs of boys that operated in and around the Jane Addams Housing Project. Before World War II the project was occupied largely by Italian residents and a few other white ethnic groups. By 1950 the black population began to increase, and by 1954 they constituted at least 50 percent of the population. As these population changes started to take place, further instability and disruption of social life started to occur. While these and other changes have an impact upon all residents of the community, they appear to affect the behavior of adolescents more directly than adults.

The old Forty-Two Gang, with its turf on Taylor Street, had disappeared. Police chases and killings were no longer common in the 1950s. The bootleggers were virtually gone. The rate of delinquency and crime had also been drastically reduced.

The Near West Side no longer had the highest rate of delinquency of the city's white population, but elements of the crime tradition continued to persist. It was also still one of the few Italian communities in the city. But there was uncertainity about the future of the Near West Side—talk of conservation, redevelopment, and urban renewal. What designs did city hall have on this area? Would the little people have a voice in any plans for its redevelopment? These questions will be discussed in Chapter 8. But these social changes are mentioned here because they exerted certain influences on our adolescents, once again giving rise to street corner groups and gangs.

To describe both the social climate of the community in the 1950s and to indicate our strategy in working with corner gangs, what follows is an account of the Kings and Knights.

THE KINGS

John Giampa started to work officially with the Hard to Reach Youth Project of the West Side Community Committee in July 1956. He had known the nucleus of the Kings almost since its inception and for that reason was employed by the project to work with them. It was in the winter of 1954 that John had become acquainted with the three boys who later formed the nucleus of the Kings. These three boys lived in the Jane Addams Housing Project, only a few blocks from John's home. He became interested in them on his own because, as he says, "I guess I started trying to do something then because they were all getting into trouble, and I didn't want to see them get into any further trouble."

John was in his mid-twenties, single, and had been born and reared on the Near West Side. When he was younger he himself had been a member of a delinquent gang. At the time of his contact with the first three boys, John was employed full time by one of the railroads. Because of his interest in underprivileged youth, he became a volunteer worker for a boys' club that was located in the basement of one of the housing project buildings. After he had served for some time in this capacity, he was asked to join the staff of the boys' club as a part-time supervisor of their game room.

The general area where members of this group lived included two distinct communities. The area surrounding the Jane Addams Housing Project was a stable Italian community where the homes were either private residences or apartments with two or more flats. There were also some mixed-usage buildings. On the whole, these buildings were physically well kept, perhaps because there was a very high percentage of resident ownership throughout this area. The families living in this community were for the most part first to third generation Americans and were examples of the Italian close-knit, stable family that participated in the affairs of the church.

The other distinct community, although separated from the former by only a street's width, was another area where members of the Kings gang resided. It was a housing project area located roughly west and south of the area of private housing just mentioned. The families who lived in the housing project were there because of financial necessity. These occupants of the low rental units of the project were recent arrivals, transients, immigrants, who for various reasons did not have an adequate income to compete for the few available rental units in the larger community.

In many cases the families of the housing project had no fathers, or the fathers could not adequately support the family. Among the Kings residing in the housing project there was not one father who contributed anything to the family. One of the mothers was on ADC (Aid to Dependent Children), and two of them worked full time. With mothers who had to work, keep house, and care for other children, these boys did not receive adequate maternal supervision and attention.

Church participation was regarded very indifferently by the Kings and their families. Although the group was almost 100 percent Catholic—the breakdown between Italian-Catholic and Mexican-Catholic being on a 19:10 ratio —only two boys attended church with their families, and one boy attended alone.

Thus, there were two distinct social strata represented in the Kings: the stable families, who were members of the private housing section of the community and ranked at least lower middle-class in regard to income and social values; and the families living in the housing project, who represented a lower economic class and a higher degree of disorganization.

The Nucleus

At the time John became acquainted with the first three Kings, their ages were 11, 12, and 13, but already they felt and often tried to act like misfits or, as they branded themselves, "rebels." Why? The school they attended, the Riis School, contained many ethnic and nationality groups. It didn't take long for children to learn that these newcomers, the "niggers," the "P. R.'s," and so forth, were a threat to them. The three boys, like those in other groups, were constantly threatened with being waylaid or getting into a "jam" (gang fight) with the enemy gang.

Living in the housing project was another source of humiliation which made them rebel. They knew why they were living in the housing project. They were living there because they had no fathers, or because the family was on relief. The feeling of being misfits or rebels could be readily seen in their reaction to the social agencies of the community. Though there were a number of recreation centers in the community, they did not regularly participate in any agency activities. When they did attend they usually wound up by being "barred out" because they would not conform.

Why were they unable to conform? John relates that in his initial efforts to introduce the boys to agencies they never fully joined wholeheartedly in any activity or program. They were either reserved and shy, huddling together in a corner—or loud, defiant and mocking. They remarked that only "fruits" went to these agencies. This was their way of saying that they were different.

Their reactions to the housing project manifested the same feelings. Window-breaking, teasing the housing project guard, congregating where the project specifically forbade loitering—in the hallways, basements, or on the roof—were the types of things they were continually doing. When the name of a housing project employee was mentioned it was usually prefixed by a curse word. Why? Because the housing project was an authority which restricted them, forced them into a pattern, required of them a definite and precise way of doing things. In their own way these boys resisted because they thought the project was to some extent responsible for their social situation.

The chief characteristic of these boys' day-to-day life was that they spent as little time at home as possible. They knew no other way to spend their time than to sit around the courtyard in the summer or in a hallway of the housing project in the winter. Card playing became a natural by-product of this idle sitting around. Usually they had no money to wager on the game; nevertheless, they spent a lot of their time in this activity, especially in summer. In the summer months, after dark, they would often sit around the court until midnight. Their mothers were either not concerned or incapable of controlling them.

For example, the boys are sitting around in the court-yard. A pie truck parks to make delivery. Soon a couple of them wander over in that direction and cunningly steal pies from the truck. Or it is around Christmas time and the department stores in the Loop and nearby neighborhood are crowded. So shoplifting excursions are the order of the day. Petty stealing from neighborhood stores is not given even a second thought.

All three boys presented truancy problems and had been brought before the family court. Any mention of the police, like the housing project authorities, was prefixed by vulgar epithets. It was a vicious cycle. Because these boys felt themselves misfits and had certain hostilities, they got into trouble; because they got into trouble with the police, the school authorities, and the housing project authorities, they felt they were being discriminated against and were therefore on the other side of the law. This situation gave added strength to their feeling of being rebels. This same cycle could be seen in their relations with the schools they attended and with the community in general.

It was evident that the boys had many traits and problems in common. They did not participate in the more accepted activities, such as athletics, as a means of gaining status, and the boy who was the most reckless in his disregard for authority, who was the most audacious and proficient in delinquent acts, was the leader of the three. This boy had to his credit such crafty cleverness as dribbling a basketball out of a Loop department store and, on another occasion, casually slinging a bow and arrow set over his shoulder and walking off with it.

Expansion and Development

The boys played with other friends and went to school with other boys, but these were just "friends"; whereas the three of them were "bosom buddies."

The community they lived in was a constant factor in their behavior. The three major ethnic and nationality groups in the housing project area were the Italians, the blacks, and the Puerto Ricans, with some Mexicans scattered here and there. Although these various groups were exposed to each other in the same school and in the same neighborhood facilities, nevertheless distinct national lines were consistently drawn, and one group always considered the other to be an actual or potential threat. Thus at school these three Italian boys were a part of the larger Italian group of boys their own age, but not of the black or Puerto Rican boys.

Within this larger group there were subgroups. The subgroups with whom the three boys eventually merged consisted of eight boys who lived in the two-block area of private residential housing that lay between the units of the Jane Addams Homes. They were known as the Fillmore Street Gang, and their ages were about the same as those of the boys from the housing project. They attended the same school, and they had common enemies. From time to time these two groups would get together for mutual protection, yet there were times when sharp lines were drawn and they threatened each other.

In the winter there were only two places to congregate: in the corridors of the housing project or in a boys' club in the basement of the housing project. The boys' club, however, had been closed to them because they had on previous occasions proved to be too disruptive to the club program.

Friction had arisen between the three boys and the Fillmore Street gang, and a fight was imminent. It was at this time that the two groups met in the boys' club—an explosive situation. That evening, however, the boys' club was having a pool tournament with another agency, and John deliberately organized the boys' club team around members of both groups, knowing that they would join even their opponents to beat an outside group. As predicted, the game went off nicely and the boys' club team was the victor; the expected "jam" was apparently forgotten.

This was the first time all these boys had been so closely associated with each other in competitive play. During the next few days boys from both groups told John, "They're pretty nice guys after you get to know them." Johnny arranged other activities which gave the boys of the two groups opportunity to get together, and after a month or two they started thinking of themselves as a single group.

An appropriate question at this point would be: Were these boys from Fillmore Street, although they came from stable homes, also misfits and rebels? This question cannot be answered by a simple yes or no. It is true that prior to the consolidation, the Fillmore Street Gang did not engage as actively in delinquent acts as did the others. However, after the merger it was evident that the boys from the housing project were generally more aggressive than those from Fillmore Street, and they set the pattern of delinquency. Although the Fillmore Street boys came from more stable homes, they were members of a larger community that was extremely aggressive and threatening, and they were also members of a boy community in which status was gained through delinquency, defying authority, and antisocial acts. In many cases the solid family background was not a sufficient deterrent to keep the boys straight.

As time went on the two groups became more solidly merged into one gang; toward the end of 1955 they started calling themselves the Kings. They tried to pattern themselves after the Knights, a gang of older boys who hung around the housing project—a group with a tough reputation, constantly in trouble with the police.

The school year 1955–56 was marked by a high rate of truancy, with about 70 percent of the boys presenting this problem. In the Christmas season of 1955, shoplifting from Loop department stores hit its peak, and most of the boys engaged in it several times a week. Engines for model railroads were the chief items they were stealing. These engines were popular with shoplifters because they were easily stolen and had a high resale potential. Other articles were stolen too, such as portable handwarmers, games, and toys. The boys sold some of these goods to other children in the community and some to a hobby shop in the Loop.

When the boys brought these stolen articles home, some of the parents were just plain gullible and accepted the boys' explanations at face value. Other parents were alarmed, but it seemed that they did little about the situation. By the spring of 1956, 9 of the 13 Kings had official records with the family court (now again called juvenile court).

What about John's role with the Kings while these events were occurring? As stated earlier, John worked part-time at the boys' club. The only time the Kings were permitted in the club was when John could personally take charge of them. Thus he spent some time with them at the club, and whatever time of his own he could spare he spent with them outside the club.

The growth of their relationship was gradual and highlighted by such things as John's interceding on their behalf with the director of the boys' club, or by letting them into the boys' club after it was officially closed so they could watch TV or play games, or taking them for a ride in his car. The boys viewed him as a good friend whom they could turn to.

In the winter of 1954 Johnny resigned his job at the railroad and was hired by the Chicago Area Project (Institute for Juvenile Research staff) to work part time handling the family court referrals. It was his role to follow up referrals of boys from the Near West Side area and to try to enlist aid from parents, relatives, or other members of the community in helping the child. Thus he became acquainted with many of the boys' parents, and the boys and their parents learned of his interest in helping them.

A rather unfortunate incident during the Christmas season of 1955 gave John unquestionable acceptance with the group. The boys asked John if he would keep the engines they had stolen in the club until they could dump them. John was not shocked by their stealing. He knew they had been doing it, since he, too, was a product of the community.

As in other incidents where he learned the boys were doing something wrong, Johnny tried to point out to them the risks and the inherent wrongness of their act without rejecting them for their behavior. After weighing the problem, Johnny told them that he would keep the engines over the weekend—this was Saturday afternoon; but that they would return them to the stores on Monday. That was the understanding. But over the weekend one of the boys was picked up by the police and implicated both the other boys and John. The police interpretation was that Johnny was "holding the stuff." It took a bit of doing to explain Johnny's role, but following this incident there was no question of Johnny's full acceptance by the boys.

At the time funds for the Hard to Reach Youth Project were to be made available, the West Side Community Committee learned that Johnny was thinking of resigning his position at the boys' club and was looking for part-time employment. He was hired for the project and assigned to work with the Kings.

In July of 1956, when the project officially began, Johnny's problem was not one of gaining acceptance by the boys but of trying to redirect them into wholesome, socially accepted activities. This turned out to be a slower process than anticipated. The chief obstacle was that the worker had developed a pattern with the boys, and it was difficult to bring about changes in it. Before, he had been able to spend only a limited amount of time with the boys, so that there had been little effort on his part to try to get them into legitimate, constructive activities.

During the summer of 1956, at about 10 o'clock in the morning, the boys would start congregating around a particular courtyard of the housing project. At noon those who did not have money would go home for lunch, and those who did would buy a hot dog at a local candy store. The greater part of the day was spent playing cards. By four or five o'clock the game would break up, and the boys would go to a nearby empty lot and play a scrape-up game of softball until supper time. After supper it was the same horsing-around, card-playing routine until 11 o'clock or midnight. About the only event which might break up this typical day was going to the movies. The boys did this a couple of times a week, more often if they could afford it.

The first thing Johnny tried to do for the boys was to get them enrolled for a week's trip at Pompeii Camp. Two of them had been there several summers earlier and had enjoyed it. This plan flopped. The boys felt that camping was sissy stuff and that they were too old for it; their average age then was about 13½. During the summer the programs at all the local agencies were either greatly curtailed or closed; thus there was no opportunity to try to introduce them to an agency program.

Johnny's task was chiefly to change from a passive role to that of an active influence on the boys' behavior, turning them towards socially approved activities. A large part of this purpose was accomplished through a sheer investment of time. Johnny could be with the boys at least five evenings a week—very often during the afternoon, too—just hanging out with them. He had little difficulty keeping them out of trouble while he was with them. His efforts to introduce them to new activities started with those with which they were familiar. He would go with them to the movies or pile some of them into his car and take them to the beach. Then he branched out with a trip to the forest preserves, swimming at Wheland Pool, and rides in the suburbs of Chicago.

Those were all new experiences for the boys. The West Side Community Committee also conducted two picnics outside the city, which the boys attended. Johnny got some interested adults in the community to drive the boys out to these affairs. Participating in a community function with adults was another new experience for them.

Toward the end of summer Johnny and a member of the community whose aid he enlisted took the boys on two overnight camping trips at Pompeii Camp. Their reactions to these trips were the usual reactions to a new experience.

Immediately after arriving on the first trip, Johnny opened up the swimming pool, but only a few of the boys went into the water. The remaining eight pulled up at the picnic table and played cards, just as if they were back at the courtyard of the housing project. Swimming out in the country was a totally new experience for many of them, so they regressed to activities in which they felt more secure.

During the summer of 1956 there was no official delinquency among the boys—and, to the best of Johnny's knowledge, no unofficial delinquency. Part of this success may be credited simply to the fact that he was constantly present, but undoubtedly he was beginning to have some positive influence on them, too. On and off during the summer they talked about starting a formal club with officers. Johnny never took sides in this issue, and they continued as a gang or as a loosely organized club.

By the fall of 1956, three of the boys were in high school, one in a parochial grammar school, and the remainder in the Riis public grammar school. The principal's regard for the boys was not too high; because many of the boys had official court records, it was evident that the Kings at Riis School were a gang, and also many of them presented truancy problems.

They felt they never got an even break from the principal and that they were marked as "eight balls." Johnny learned that Sister Honora, principal and teacher of a local parochial school, was interested in enrolling boys who were presenting such problems. Johnny consulted with the boys' parents, and within a month after the beginning of the school year transfers were arranged for all the Kings. We did not pass judgment on this step; they seemed to present much less of a behavior problem at this new school, and truancy decreased, though it did not disappear.

In the fall, the local parks and agencies resumed their full programs, and Johnny started talking to the boys about participating in some of them. He tried for a month subtly to direct them into one agency or another, but to no avail. They would either come right out and say that these places were just for "fruits" or would find one excuse or another for not going.

In the meantime it was becoming more and more evident that the boys regarded Johnny as a leader, a factor which he began to exploit. One day with no warning he told them: "I've made some arrangements. On Tuesday we're going down to the boys' club to work in the craft room. On Thursday we'll watch the movies they show at the Western Avenue Branch." No dissenting. No gripes. A program was instituted, one which the boys seemed to enjoy. This was just the beginning. When they went to these agencies, they did not mix. They had to do things in an exclusive group. But in time. . . .

Johnny noted that in the spring of 1956 the boys began to notice the girls who hung around the same courtyard. Mary became Billy's girl. There were about eight of these girls, of about the same age as the Kings, all living in the housing project. As Johnny became increasingly active with the Kings, the girls began to become envious of the boys' club and their activities. These girls, much the same as the boys, were presenting a potentially serious behavior problem. Their language was already almost as foul as that of the boys, and their sexual activities were threatening to become promiscuous. In September 1956, the West Side Community Committee's Hard to Reach Youth Project assigned a young woman to work with them. The boys and girls became involved in planning some social activities together.

Another problem was gang fights. In September 1956, a gang fight was threatening between the Kings and another gang. A couple of the Kings contacted Johnny and said, "Johnny, the guys are gonna jam on Grenshaw Street. Let's call up Denato and have him bust it up before it starts."

Officer Denato was a black juvenile officer. Johnny had become acquainted with him some time earlier and had introduced him on an informal basis to the boys. After the boys got to know him they would wave to him when he drove by, and they felt that he was their friend. One of the boys put it this way: "You know, Johnny, he doesn't act like a nigger or a cop." Johnny, in a similar manner, introduced other friends of his who were members of minority groups. Thus hostilities toward minority groups and the police lessened.

Formerly, calls to the police by neighbors and the housing project complaining that the Kings were causing a disturbance were fairly frequent. However, Johnny's role developed into that of a liaison. If members of the community had complaints regarding the boys, they handled them through Johnny. Johnny in turn tried to interpret the boys' behavior to members of the community. Meetings of the Kings were held at which the guard and other housing project officials were present.

Johnny continued working with the Kings for the next two years in the manner described. Movement was not always forward. There were many setbacks. Some of the boys continued to be truant, caused disturbances, and engaged in minor thefts. However, none of these activities at this time resulted in police action or court appearances.

Over half of the boys dropped out of high school and secured employment. The others went to work upon graduating. With continued direction, the boys began to occupy more meaningful roles and gradually became incorporated into the conventional life of the community.

THE KNIGHTS

The Knights numbered about 35 members, who ranged in age from 15 to 20, with most about 16½ years. Sixteen members had family court records. Fifteen of them were unofficial delinquents—that is, they had not been caught. Their juvenile offenses included assaults, sex charges, truancy, jackrolling, shoplifting, and stealing cars.

Not one of the gang had graduated from high school. Five attended regular city and parochial schools, five were at Montefiore Special School, and the remaining four attended Logan Continuation School one day a week. Of these 14, ten planned to quit school as soon as they reached 17, the age required in Illinois law.

This gang dated from the days when most of them were attending the same grade school. They were a play group that hung out in a courtyard of the ABLA Housing Project, a large, 4,000-unit, half-square mile, low rent, public housing area on Roosevelt Road. ("ABLA" is an abbreviation referring to four housing projects in this vicinity: the Jane Addams, the Brooks, the Loomis Courts, and Abbott Homes. The Knights actually hung out in the Jane Addams Housing Project, a 1,000-unit project.) As black families began to move in and their children started playing in the couryards, friction arose between the black children and the Knights, who moved their hangout north, to a housing project courtyard on Taylor Street. The group that moved north numbered about 15 boys, 11 of whom were Italian, three Mexican, and one Irish. Here, along Taylor Street, they combined with another, largely Italian group of about ten boys they had known at school. But before they gave up the courtyard on Roosevelt, they protested their ouster by breaking the windows.

Frank, the natural leader of the group from Roosevelt, again emerged as the leader when they combined with the group on Taylor Street. Frank lived on Racine Avenue just off Taylor Street. He was 5' 9" tall and weighed about 140 pounds—not a big chap. His grandfather had immigrated from Italy around the turn of the century and had settled on the Near West Side. During the 1920s, Frank's father,

Tony, then in his teens, made an occasional dollar by selling bootleg whiskey; but later he started peddling produce from a wagon, then from a truck, and after that had a thriving produce business. Tony's idea of the law was, "Everybody's got their hand out." Frank's older brother spent a couple of years in jail on an armed robbery charge.

Frank himself instigated and led the Knights in many delinquent activities. Starting about 1954, when these boys were 14 and 15 years of age, but man-size, they were engaged regularly in jackrolling. Friday night—pay day—was always jackrolling night. Frank would designate which boys would engage the drunk in conversation, which ones were to assault him, and who was to lift his money. Some of the assaults were brutal and sadistic. Often, after they knocked a man down they would work him over with their feet.

When Frank's brother was sent to jail, his family insisted that it was a bum rap. When Frank, who had been drinking at a party, stole a car, got into an accident with it, left the scene of the accident, and was caught by the police, his father bribed the police to drop the charges. What respect did Frank have for the law? Very little.

And how much respect did the other boys have for the law and the police? One day a motorcycle policeman pulled up at the courtyard where the Knights hung out, got off his motorcycle and started telling them that he had just been assigned to the community. He said they weren't going to pull any fast stuff on him as they had on other police because he had grown up in the neighborhood. While he was talking to them, one of the Knights lifted his keys from his belt. He gave chase, but to no avail, and the group openly ridiculed him. It was only through the intervention of the worker assigned to the Knights, who happened by, that the keys were returned.

These were the boys Frank Gabitz was introduced to in the spring of 1956. Gabitz, who had grown up in the neighborhood, at that time lived a few blocks west and knew only a few of them. He was 34 and single. While attending high school he had joined one of the Near West Side's many storefront social and athletic clubs and later became its president. In 1942 he was drafted and served in the air corps until his discharge in 1945. After his return from the service he resumed his membership in the social-athletic club. He attended Roosevelt College for a couple of years and then worked as a bookkeeper. In 1950 he was recalled to the air corps for service in Korea. In the interval between 1945 and 1950, the West Side Community Committee gave impetus to and sponsored the Inter-Club Council (see Chapter 5). Gabitz was an officer in one of the clubs, the club's representative to the council, and soon became the council's president.

Most of the social and athletic clubs that originated when the boys were in their teens (many survived to have members in their 40s and 50s) needed an adult sponsor to handle their business affairs, such as the signing of a lease for a storefront clubroom, contracting for balls and bands, and so forth. Thus Gabitz, who was seen as a capable leader, was asked to serve as sponsor to three such well-structured social-athletic clubs prior to his recall to the military in 1950.

Upon his discharge in 1952, Gabitz went to work for the West Side Community Committee, holding various positions of responsibility, including that of staff member at their summer camp, promoter of a fund-raising drive, and editor of a local newspaper.

At the beginning of 1956, when it was learned that funds would be made available to the West Side Community Committee by the Hard to Reach Youth Project, the delinquency committee quickly indicated that the Knights should receive priority in being assigned a worker. The Knights were often discussed by this committee, who wished to extend some aid to them because of their disruptiveness in the community. Thus, in March 1956, Gabitz was assigned by the West Side Community Committee to work with the Knights, and in July of that year his work with the WSCC became a part-time job while he devoted the rest of his time to the Knights under the Hard to Reach Youth Project.

At the time of Gabitz's introduction to the Knights they were looking for a sponsor; they wanted a clubroom. Their average age at that time was about 16. Johnny Giampa, who was already affiliated with the Kings, learned of their wish for a sponsor and told them that he had a friend who might be willing to serve in that capacity. They were a little skeptical. "Who in hell would want to sponsor us?" they asked Johnny. "We've got a rotten reputation."

The introduction was cautiously arranged. About three weeks were purposely allowed to slip by before Gabitz was introduced, during which time the boys kept asking Johnny when he was going to bring his buddy around—or had his buddy chickened out? Johnny assured them that as soon as his friend found some time he would be around. Finally, Johnny said that this young man could make it the next night, and that he wanted them all to meet him at the Jane Addams Boys Club facility in the basement room of the housing project.

The Knights were there in full force that night, and Johnny introduced Gabitz. A few of the boys knew him casually from seeing him around the neighborhood. Most of them knew, through his association with the other community clubs which he sponsored, that the "Gabitz Clubs" all had well-furnished clubrooms, threw good dances, and were generally well organized.

Gabitz was well prepared for this introduction. He had made inquiries from neighborhood people who knew these boys and had investigated their court records. He knew that Frank was their leader not by virtue of being the biggest or toughest but because he was shrewd; he had never been brought before the family court, he had natural leadership qualities, and he was extremely aggressive. He also knew that Frank extracted a tax from the other boys for his leadership. He would collect "dues" for club jackets or a party, and the money would never be accounted for.

For a worker to revamp a group's structure and to transfer it from a gang to a formal club on the first evening he met with them seemed too fast, but Gabitz called for an election of officers. He explained that if he was to be their sponsor they would have to conduct themselves as a regular club, not like a gang of rowdies.

In evaluating the instant acceptance of a formal club structure, the following should be kept in mind: the boys wanted a storefront clubroom, they knew that Gabitz sponsored formal clubs, and they distrusted their own leader. In addition there was the worker's practical need for a structure to be of service to this large, 35-member group. Gabitz knew it was inevitable that the boys would elect Frank as their president because of their combined fear and respect of him, yet he was also aware that they distrusted him. Therefore he structured the election to provide for a board of five governors to whom the officers had to account and who had power to impeach the president. The boys liked this idea, and it was instituted.

Gabitz gained acceptance with the group in fairly short order. He showed them in tangible ways that he could help them. Regular meetings were scheduled to be held at the local CYO, an agency from which the Knights had been banned because of their disruptive influence and into which they were allowed only under Gabitz's supervision. For a long time the boys had been wanting to throw a dance, but under Frank's leadership it never materialized. With Gabitz's stimulus, the Knights gave a dance at Our Lady of Pompeii Church. A great many similar dances given by teenage clubs had turned out to be not much more than brawls, but Gabitz urged the boys to try to run a good clean dance, one to which they could invite their parents.

The dance went off smoothly. The Knights watched like hawks for anyone trying to sneak in liquor. Many of the parents did, in fact, come. Invitations were also accepted by the juvenile officers of the Maxwell Street Station and the two local probation officers. With the funds realized from this dance, the boys placed a down-payment on club sweaters.

In the discussion of this group with the supervisory staff of the West Side Community Committee, the question arose as to whether, at this late stage, anything could be done to change some of the Knights' negative values. At the beginning, Gabitz remained somewhat aloof from the boys, showing up only at meetings, serving in the capacity of a consultant, and making some suggestions. Gradually he started hanging out with them in the courtyard. Then he arranged a basketball period for them at the CYO.

There was no drastic curtailment of the Knights' delinquent activities during the spring and early summer of 1956. The only decrease of delinquent acts which could definitely be attributed to the worker's influence during this period was that the boys, out of respect for Gabitz, would not engage in delinquent acts in his presence. This point is illustrated by Gabitz's report in June, 1956:

> We were sitting around the Wall [the wall in the courtyard of the housing project]. It was about eleven at night. Eight or nine of the Knights were there, and four of the girls. A couple of Puerto Ricans, probably in their mid-twenties, walked by. Mitchell said, loud enough for the Puerto Ricans to hear, "Let's jump 'em." The Puerto Ricans started running, and the boys who were playing cards dropped their cards and got ready to chase them. I stopped them and said, "Where the hell do you think you're going?" I then did something that I rarely do—I told them that I was really disgusted and ashamed of them and lectured them in general.
>
> This is the first time anything of this sort has happened in my presence. Often the boys would say, "If you weren't

here, Gabitz, we'd do so and so." And I know that un-
provoked assaults of this sort are occasionally conducted by
the boys, especially against Negroes and Puerto Ricans. On
Monday, May 14, about 10 o'clock at night, Johnny Giampa
and I were riding down Taylor Street. We saw a large crowd
near the Tastee Freeze on Taylor and Lytle Street. We asked
Vito what happened, and he told us that a bunch of Knights
were being held at the Maxwell Street Police Station because
of a fight. We drove them to the station and talked with
Officer Denato (the juvenile officer with whom the HTRYP
of the WSCC had a very good relationship).

The story, as related by Denato, and as I later learned
from the boys, is this: Earlier that evening Louis, one of the
Knights, had an argument with a Negro boy near the Wall,
and a fight started. Some grown-ups broke up the fight. The
Negro boy left but later returned in a car with three other
boys. They were evidently looking for Louis. About this time
approximately eight or ten Knights, including Louis, were
congregated near the Wall. One of the Negro boys got out
of the car and started walking over toward Louis. The
Knights immediately rushed the three Negro boys. One of
the Negro boys pulled out a knife, and it was taken away
from him. During the fight the Knights broke the windows
of the car, a 1956 Ford, and ripped up the upholstery.

When I arrived at the Wall, I noticed a number of cars
with Knights in them pulling away from the curb. A few girls
were also in the cars. One of the girls yelled out for me to
follow them, that they were going to fight some boys from
18th Street. About 15 minutes later the boys returned, and
I learned what happened. The boys were standing around
near the Wall when two of the girls came by in a car. They
were excited and told the boys they were riding down 18th
Street when a group of boys "rapped" at them (made insult-
ing remarks). The girls yelled to the 18th Street group that
they would be back with their friends. When the girls came
to the Wall, they were determined to have the Knights go to
18th Street and avenge them.

At first the boys did not react to their pleas, but when
the girls started calling them chicken, Fred and Sam answered the challenge and the rest of the boys followed. A
couple of the other girls went and rounded up members of
two more groups. When all converged on 18th Street in

> their cars, there were about 25 boys. As soon as the group
> of boys on 18th Street saw them arrive, they started running.
> Only four of them were caught. The Knights and their co-
> horts knocked them down, then stomped on them. These
> four boys were in pretty bad shape, I understand.

During the warm months of the summer and spring a few of the Knights were always hanging out in a particular courtyard of the housing project along Taylor Street. Most of the Knights were working during the summer, but in the evening they would be in the courtyard, anywhere from 5 to 20 boys on any given evening. A brick wall of a convenient height for sitting or lounging was recognized as the exclusive hangout of the Knights, and their right to that section was respected. The Knights painted their name in fairly large letters on this wall. During the day things were quiet. During the evening the boys, all under age, would buy beer and drink it openly at the wall. They drank and played cards there.

Delinquent acts such as stealing car accessories, shoplifting, and vandalism against housing project property served to diversify their evenings. The pattern was determined by the "heat" that the police exerted and on how badly the boys needed money. Strangely enough, in their jackrolling activities they did not consider themselves criminals. They considered it all in the nature of mischief and an easy way to get money. Anyway, the men who were assaulted were usually blacks or Puerto Ricans, so the boys figured it didn't matter much. It was not until the end of the summer, when the father of one of the Knights was jackrolled and badly beaten, that the nature of their acts came home to them and they seemed to have decided to stop this activity.

By June, Gabitz was spending five or six nights a week hanging out with the Knights. He found it impossible to try to spend time with all the members equally. He therefore decided to concentrate on the leaders of the gang, with attention to such other boys as he felt especially needed it, and through them he tried to influence the club as a whole.

Stock-car races, for which Gabitz obtained tickets, became a regular weekly activity. He introduced Frank, the leader of the Knights, and four or five other boys to tennis and horseback riding. Fishing was another activity that many of the boys had never tried before. Gabitz developed a regular group that went fishing quite often during the summer. His hope of getting them organized into a softball league never materialized, but they did play softball against other community teams. Gabitz took the boys on two week-end camping trips at Pompeii Camp.

All summer long the boys had been talking about a storefront clubroom. They knew that Gabitz would have to sign the lease. He warned them that he had seen too many clubs break up because of the financial pressure caused by having to pay rent. Gabitz was afraid of their drinking and bringing girls into the clubroom, but they were deter-mined.

They raised the dues to $1.25 a week and ran raffles. By the end of the summer they had about $300 in the treasury. Again they confronted Gabitz, and this time he felt that he had to go along with them. Furniture was brought in (a few stolen items), walls were painted, and in mid-September the Knights moved into their clubroom. It was tastefully decorated; they had a TV set, a pop dis-penser, couches, chairs, a couple of card tables, and a bar they had built.

The clubroom instantly accomplished one thing: it took the boys off the street. During the first two weeks, card playing was the main activity of the club. Pots amounting to $100 were not uncommon, and the "house" (the club) took 10 percent of every pot. But as the novelty of playing cards for big stakes wore off, the card games became less popular, with only four or five boys continuing to play habitually. The others would watch TV or lounge around.

When the club had to make decisions, Gabitz always remained in the background, exerting his influence subtly, prior to meetings. But in establishing house rules, he directly asserted himself in two areas. He explained to the boys that since he was their sponsor and the lease was in his name, anything that went wrong in the club was a reflection on him. He therefore insisted that no liquor or women should be brought into the clubroom. Girls would be allowed in only for parties and on certain Saturday open-house days. Delinquent acts practically stopped while the Knights were in their clubroom. They now had some place to go, and they were afraid that if they became involved in a gang fight the plate-glass windows of the store would be an excellent target for retaliation by an enemy gang.

There were about eight girls associated with the Knights; when the Knights started hanging out at the Wall on Taylor Street, this group of girls, who lived in that area, started hanging out with them. Of Italian descent, they were on the average about 1½ years younger than the Knights. They soon began to consider themselves the sister club of the Knights and called themselves the Knights Auxiliary, although they had no formal structure; nor were they officially recognized by the boys.

Only two of these girls went steady with members of the Knights. The rest just hung around. Occasionally one of the boys would take one of them out, but that was a rare exception. They dressed boyishly in levis and tried to act hardened. The boys never changed their topic of conversation for the sake of the girls nor curtailed their use of vulgarities. Perhaps their presence even encouraged the boys to discuss their sexual exploits with other girls. The girls never seemed to be embarrassed by this freedom of speech and were fully capable of their own vulgarities, which often matched those of the boys. Sexual liberties with these girls were, for the most part, restricted to a sort of horsing around.

When the Knights moved into the clubroom the girls felt left out. On several occasions they showed resentment by trying to get the boys involved in gang fights, but the boys weren't biting.

Several of the boys who had been in the service were expected home for Thanksgiving, and the Knights began thinking of a party. They insisted on having liquor. Gabitz was in a dilemma. Finally he told them that if they decided to have liquor, he would have nothing to do with the party. Gabitz withdrew and did not help the boys with any of their arrangements. On the night of the party he dropped in for a few minutes about 9:30. Some of the boys were pretty drunk, but things were fairly well in hand.

When he dropped back about one in the morning the party was over, and two members who had stayed to clean things up were just getting ready to leave. From them and others during the next few days, Gabitz learned what had transpired. The liquor was delivered in the afternoon, and the boys started drinking then. By ten in the evening most of them were pretty drunk, and the party was starting to get loud and rowdy. The police came around and told them to break it up.

One of the girls, Bill's date, was pretty intoxicated. One of the other members sneaked her out of the clubroom to his car. Bill, missing his girl and suspecting what had happened, went to look for her. He found her in this boy's car almost unconscious and about to be sexually assaulted. A bitter fight ensued. Bill drove the girl home. About an hour later an ambulance drove up to her home and she was taken to the hospital. Narcotics, among other things, were suspected as the cause of her illness, though it turned out to be a matter only of excessive drinking.

Gabitz, along with the rest of the club members, spent some very anxious moments when rumor had it that the girl was in a critical condition. Gabitz was thoroughly disgusted and very disappointed by this incident. He entertained the idea of giving up his work with the Knights, but in time and with encouragement he decided to stay with them.

After the party the financial pressure of monthly rent —the dues had been upped to $2 a week—began to tell. Many of the boys were in arrears in their dues. Rifts and cliques developed within the club, and on December 1 the clubroom was abandoned. By the end of 1956, the Knights had broken up into cliques, and Gabitz concentrated on the younger clique, although he kept in contact with all the boys, dropping in on them at their various hangouts. He began to encourage the younger group, with some success, to participate in the programs of the Jane Addams Boys Club, and twice a week, with tickets furnished through the West Side Community Committee, he took them to hockey games, basketball games, or boxing matches.

These activities continued during the next two years. Then members of the Knights began to grow up; gradually most of them got jobs, some moved out of the area, a few had subsequent arrest records, and a few got married. Thus was repeated here, as with most adolescents, the matura-tion process; the adolescent begins to have opportunities for occupying constructive roles and gradually joins con-ventional life.

How effective was the Hard to Reach Youth Project, in our community and elsewhere? Like all delinquency pre-vention programs, this one was not a phenomenal success, but it did represent a breakthrough, a new thrust into the social world of street corner groups that a large number of adolescents belonged to and still belong to. In the case of the Kings and the Knights, we believe that our intervention reduced gang fights, curtailed delinquency, aided many of the members with their personal problems, provided new types of constructive experiences, and redirected some of their energies away from the streets and into the conven-tional institutions of the community. The assignment of a worker to gangs such as these, in my opinion, was profitable enough to warrant this type of intervention. At any rate, the use of indigenous leaders like John Giampa, or the "detached workers" with college training, provided by various agencies, continues to be a technique employed in youth work, and these procedures are likely to be carried on in the years ahead as one means of maintaining communication with hostile, alienated youth.

THE COMING OF DRUGS

Until 1945 the problem of drug abuse was virtually nonexistent in our community. Then suddenly, after the war, marijuana and heroin became widespread. By the early 1950s it had become a problem in our immediate neighborhood, and it had reached almost epidemic proportions in the adjoining black area and throughout the inner city areas of Chicago. The highest concentration of heroin addicts seemed to come from the Jane Addams Housing Project. They congregated in the vicinity of Laflin and Lexington. They were adolescents and young adults whose families were of low socioeconomic status and had many social problems.

Why should so many drugs suddenly plague our neighborhood and, especially, a large number of black communities in Chicago? Why did drug addiction become a social phenomenon? To begin with, drugs became available for the first time on an unprecedented scale. Dope peddlers and pushers found it easy and very profitable to sell marijuana and heroin to young people looking for kicks. The most fertile soil for distribution of drugs was street corners in black areas or in neighborhoods undergoing social changes. Middle-class areas were little aware of the problem at the time; but narcotic use has now, of course, become commonplace there, too.

What should community workers do when they encountered adolescents on drugs? Some of these kids came to our center for assistance. The workers would listen to their problems and try to understand and give some guidance. Some of them could be helped in this way, but reaching those hooked on heroin was terribly frustrating. John Giampa, our community worker, relates the following experiences:

Trying to help kids who were on dope was one of the most difficult problems I had to deal with in the late 1940s and ever since. I despaired many times as I saw kids looking for kicks, many of them dying from the experience. I remember Anthony B., who started with marijuana after he came back from Korea. For ten years he was on heroin. He stole from home, from work when he had a job, and from houses and stores. Finally his brain became damaged. He would go to the cemetery and cry out, "I want to die." And finally, after becoming like a vegetable, he had a massive stroke and died.

Dope was pushed in the schools in the early 1950s, and there was peer-group pressure to experiment. Some kids felt that they had to try it to be considered one of the gang. I used to have a lot of rap sessions with the kids right on the corner. I would listen to their problems and do some individual counseling. I remember one kid who was in very bad shape—all mixed up emotionally. It was a tough task to get him to go to a psychiatrist, but he finally did; and he finally made it.

By 1960 the problem decreased in our community. Perhaps some of our community programs had a little effect, but I also believe that good police work helped a great deal. There was Officer Bernard Brown, for instance, who had real understanding, knew the community, and succeeded in breaking up the dope ring in the area.

However, by 1963 drugs again were in wide use. Marijuana, LSD, speed, uppers, downers, and other barbituates were introduced to neighborhood kids. In 1965 a girl died almost in my arms. Her mother called me at 1:30 A.M. for help. The girl was screaming hysterically. We called an ambulance, but she died shortly after at the University of Illinois hospital.

Giampa's experience was a forerunner of a problem which has become increasingly prevalent and urgent. This problem has been dealt with by our committee and other agencies by the street work techniques we pioneered.

Part III

THE NEIGHBORHOOD AND THE CITY

There's a college campus on the site now. I call my neighborhood the Circle Campus parking lot. That's all we are for
the campus and the medical center. Our streets are choked
with cars. Perhaps the college performs a needed function.
Yet there is nothing quite beautiful about the thing. It's
walled off from the community. Jane Addams was against
walls that separate people. She believed in a neighborhood
with all kinds of people. She wondered if it couldn't be
extended to the world.

Florence Scala

Chapter 8

REDEVELOPING A NEIGHBORHOOD

Although the Near West Side Community Committee and the Chicago Area Project have been successful in improving the lives and the environments of many individuals, we have been less successful in preventing governmental and industrial forces from making large-scale changes in the area and thus in the lives of the many individuals who live there.

What follows is a detailed story of the partial destruction and renewal of the Near West Side. It is only partly a success story, but keep in mind that organizations that have made it their explicit goal to combat such forces have not had much success either. Even though the goals of some militant community organizations have been to modify basic social conditions and hopefully to improve housing and the physical environment, spectacular results have not been achieved. Many of these forces are citywide and spread throughout the fabric of our society.

Notwithstanding these difficulties, we believe that our leadership was in the right direction. The fact that we did not reach all our objectives is not a refutation of our cardinal principle: it is indispensible in planning for the improvement of the community that local residents and indigenous leaders be actively involved and assume primary responsibility.

EARLY PROSPECTS

Early in 1948, farsighted members of our committee became aware of the new planning developments in the area. On the west, the medical center was buying land; on the north, the Congress Street superhighway was underway; on the east, another part of the highway system was to be constructed; and in the Canalport and South Side areas of the city, community groups were making plans for redevelopment of their neighborhoods. In 1947, several bills had been passed by the state legislature designed as a comprehensive and realistic solution to the housing crisis. The Blighted Areas Redevelopment Act provided for the purchase of land in blighted areas by the Land Clearance Commission, a public municipal corporation, and the construction of housing on this land primarily by private investors. The Non-Profit Housing Act provided that this commission and the housing authority could apply to the state housing board for funds. The Relocation Housing Act provided for the rehousing, by the housing authority, of low-income families displaced by demolition and removal of buildings under the Blighted Areas Redevelopment Act.

Also at this time, bond issues were passed by the voters of Chicago, which, when added to federal, state, and local funds on hand at that time, made more than $55 million available for redevelopment. It was obvious that these laws could benefit the Near West Side, and that this money plus private capital could result in new homes, more parks and schools, and better business and industrial facilities. It seemed certain that the Near West Side would get some of this redevelopment money because of its nearness to the Loop and its central location with respect to jobs, and it was the belief of many planning and housing officials that new investments would be attracted near existing redevelopment areas such as Michael Reese Hospital or the Illinois Institute of Technology on the South Side, or the new medical center adjacent to the Near West Side.

Forward-looking people began to feel that if the community itself did not influence its future development, the residential population would resume its prewar flight from the area on an increased scale after the housing shortage lessened. With further deterioration, business and industry would find it increasingly difficult to attract customers and employees. In the absence of planning, the rebuilding that might occur would be piecemeal, would diminish existent investments, and would deflect future ones.

In the light of these conditions it seemed clear that to improve residential, community, and commercial-industrial facilities, the Near West Side needed some schemes of organization that would make the best use of its resources and the advantages of its location. It was thought necessary to establish a plan that would, over the years, insure orderly growth influenced by and of benefit to present residents and business people of the area. Because our plans ultimately had such an unexpected and instructive fate, let me go into some details about our efforts.

THE PLANNING BOARD

Hull House was asked by a delegation of West Side Community Committee members to arrange some discussions on redevelopment. A number of luncheon meetings were held. They were attended by businessmen, industrialists, laymen, and community workers and leaders. They agreed that the community should itself plan its reconstruction and do it democratically, with everyone participating, before outside interests decided what was to be done and before money was wasted on piece-meal building.

At these informal discussions the group developed keen interest in replanning the area, and it set up, informally, a Temporary Organizing Committee for Redevelopment of the Near West Side to open the subject to interested people in the area without dominating any organization that might result from their work. At the direction of the temporary committee, Mr. Russell Ballard, the director of Hull House, on October 1, 1948, sent its statement of purpose to residents of the area, asking them to join the group in the creation of an organization to plan for redevelopment.

Further discussions by the temporary committee were directed by Eri Hulbert. Eri Hulbert was Jane Addams's nephew. As the executive director of the Near West Side Planning Board, he later became responsible for a great deal of the planning for redeveloping our neighborhood during the first ten years. When he died in 1959, this function was taken over by the several agencies of city government mentioned in this chapter.

Hulbert's services were made available by Hull House. They led to the committee's formulation of the following three things which they deemed necessary for redevelopment:

1. *A representative community organization to raise money for making a plan.* The group meeting at Hull House did not propose to solicit or receive money immediately but wished first to form an organization representative of the total community which would set itself up legally to work out a program and to promote and finance a planning board.

2. *A planning board and staff to make the plan.* We believed that a planning body is the only method of achieving orderly rebuilding and growth and avoiding decay, piecemeal construction, and wrong guesses by private investors. It stresses the overall view needed to harmonize and interrelate the various kinds of interests people hold. Its value and success depend on its ability to deal effectively with these interests by establishing and maintaining constant contacts with residents and business people in the area and with city housing and planning agencies, by explaining various proposals and modifying these proposals as the community desires. In this manner it directs the planning staff toward the ultimate goals to be achieved. Its unique work of developing overall plans duplicates no other organization but supplements the work of all organizations and gives them a reliable framework for their particular efforts. We discussed the difference between a planning board whose work would be followed by redevelopment by a combination of other agencies interested in rebuilding according to plan and a planning board which would be merely a necessary step in the formation of a specific redevelopment corporation. The former was recommended.

3. *Redevelopment organizations to carry out the plan.* When a general plan had been evolved and accepted, public and private organizations and individual investment in residential, community, commercial, and industrial facilities would build according to plan, together creating a new Near West Side. The area of concentration was west of the Chicago River, south of Congress Street (later renamed the Eisenhower Expressway), east of Ashland Avenue, and north of the 16th Street tracks. We believed that no community in the nation had ever created a practical vision of its future with the participation of every kind of person, group, and interest. The people of the Near West Side saw the opportunity to be the first to demonstrate that democracy can function in remaking the world they live in. Here was a new

frontier for courageous people with a pioneering spirit. Here was the possibility of a new community for people with a real pride in the place where they live, work, and play. In the words of the Temporary Committee, "Only by planning now can the area keep its population, business and industry, and make a new Near West Side."

By December 1949 the Near West Side Planning Board was a reality. It moved quickly to help people organize some action programs for the immediate future. The people of the Near West Side had been confused by countless rumors about the possibility of various redevelopment programs for the community; therefore several meetings were held and a number of measures applied to inform residents of the problem and get them to work on improving the community.

Most of the people in the area bounded by Harrison Street, Roosevelt Road, Halsted Street, and Ashland Boulevard desired a continued community life on the Near West Side, and in the eyes of the members of the Near West Side Planning Board they were entitled to it. The Planning Board felt that the people of the community could do a good job of rebuilding, including the raising of necessary funds; and they opposed the ouster of large numbers of people by large-scale housing development imposed from the outside. They felt that if all the people of the community—residents, landlords, political officials, clergymen, and public and private agencies—would support a self-help program of improvement and rebuilding, they could then be assured of continued residence.

In their efforts to impress upon the people of the Near West Side the importance of the planning board program, the *Community News,* a local newspaper published by the West Side Community Committee, presented an article in its issue of December 1949 in which it urged landlords and tenants alike to unite to keep their community. The article described the effects which a land clearance and redevelopment project would have on them. Landlords would receive actual value for their property, and they would have to move and purchase other property elsewhere at inflated values; while tenants would be unable to find housing elsewhere which they could afford.

To induce the Land Clearance Commission to make recommendations favorable for residents of the Near West Side to improve their own community, the West Side Community Committee, in the same article, urged each landlord to sign a petition which would state that if his property would not be condemned he would cooperate in every effort to improve it and, if necessary, repair it, so that it would meet proper standards.

The West Side Community Committee, instrumental in starting the planning board itself, played an important role in pushing certain action programs. They agreed to take responsibility for block by block rehabilitation and conservation programs in the area bounded by Roosevelt Road, Ashland Boulevard, Congress Street, and Halsted Street, and to meet with the Land Clearance Commission to find out its plans for redevelopment. Three large committees—on community organization services, on planning, and on coordination with outside agencies—were set up by the West Side Community Committee to attack the problem of abandoned buildings in the area, to investigate possibilities for block redevelopment, to study a proposal of the Western Society of Engineers for industrial development of an area east of Halsted Street, to work on the enforcement of minimum housing standards, to get community cooperation on neighborhood housekeeping, and to investigate an immediate proposal for the establishment of some off-street parking for the use of businessmen in the area.

On November 22, 1949, members of the Near West Side Planning Board met with the Chicago Land Clearance

Commission to discuss the commission's survey of the Near West Side. (Established by the City of Chicago, the commission was the predecessor agency of the Department of Urban Renewal.) One of the objectives of the planning board was to save existing buildings wherever possible. The commission was asked what its attitude was on these points and how it could help the planning board accomplish these objectives.

The commission expressed sympathy with any plan by which the people could help themselves, but felt that verbal assurances were not sufficient and wanted a definite program that would include plans for the necessary financing. In the event that any clearance would be done, the commission expressed interest in dealing with the property owners themselves. In connection with its survey, the commission stated that to clear any area it must first assemble the facts and then make a recommendation. At the time of this meeting the commission had made no recommendation, but it expected to make one soon. If clearance would be judged necessary and the community could organize to rebuild, the commission expressed interest in assisting with such a plan. The survey information gathered by the commission was to be made available to the planning board immediately.

The planning board pointed out that time was needed to mobilize the interest of the people, and it agreed to begin at once on some plans for rehabilitation and conservation and to explore possibilities for an adequately financed redevelopment plan. The commission offered the members of the planning board a great deal of encouragement in their aims, pointing out the advantages of the area, agreeing that grassroots organization was the key to community improvement, and urging them to begin at once on their program.

On November 29, 1949, in conference with the directors of the Near West Side Planning Board, the members of the housing committee of the West Side Community Committee set out a program for immediate action to demonstrate to the Land Clearance Commission that the people of the community wanted to remain there and help rebuild it; and they produced a plan whereby mass clearance and eviction of present residents by the Land Clearance Commission could be avoided.

On December 7, 1949, the following decisions were made. The aforementioned petition asking for their support for a community improvement program would be circulated to all property owners and then presented to the Land Clearance Commission. The West Side Community Committee was to continue its efforts in mapping home ownership, accumulating information about property, and assembling the material made available by the Land Clearance Commission. The chairman of the housing committee was to contract authorities regarding the destruction of the first abandoned building, after which the director of the Catholic Youth Organization Center and the director of Hull House were to work with a committee on the other abandoned buildings. School principals were to be asked to report where "Go Slow" traffic signs and white lines down the middle of the streets were necessary to protect schoolchildren going to and from the schools. On receipt of this information, the appropriate city authorities were to be contacted.

A letter was to be sent by the planning board signed by the chairman of the house committee to the alderman of the ward requesting street lights on Norton Street between Harrison and Polk Streets. The planning board was to determine which city agency was responsible for "No Parking" signs at street corners where streetcars and buses stopped, and the appropriate agency would be contacted so that these signs might be obtained where needed. Selection of blocks for rehabilitation was to be made when the Land

Clearance Commission survey information was properly assembled and ready for use.

During this period the finance committee of the Near West Side Planning Board was meeting and putting its efforts into securing allocations from industry and business in the area. The committee on membership met on December 12 to put into effect a program for spreading information about the planning board and securing participation in the work of other committees for improving the community.

The Near West Side Planning Board, with the West Side Community Committee the most active among many cooperating agencies, spent the next two years attempting to determine some of the reasons for the community's deterioration and to establish methods of renovation. The planning board was interested in facts about how land was used, how streets were used, conditions of all other types of buildings, and the relationship of the community to the rest of Chicago. In other words, the planning board was interested in all the physical conditions in the industrial, business, and residential sections of the area. And it was interested in formulating a method of changing these conditions based on a reliable plan for the future.

Determining all the facts, reaching decisions, and making a plan required several years of unceasing effort, but by June 1951 the planning board presented its report to the community in an article in the *Community News,* stating the results of extensive studies of the area and proposals for the future based on them.

PROBLEMS AND PRINCIPLES

The area was characterized as one of the most important in Chicago: there were fifty thousand residents, some fifteen hundred small-business people, and three or four

hundred larger businesses and industries within its bound-
aries. It is close to downtown Chicago and Lake Michigan
and is situated in the front yard of the medical center, which
by 1949 had renovated several blocks of old, long-neg-
lected buildings typical of so many others to be found in the
blighted areas of the Near West Side. To cope with the
housing shortage, the medical center Commission refurnished three groups of buildings at a comparatively low
cost, offering clean, decent living quarters. The results
demonstrated the possibilities of reclaiming blighted
neighborhoods when concerted action by owners could be
organized.

Also included in the area studied by the Near West
Side Planning Board were important and valuable railroad
tracks along the east and south and the Congress Street
Expressway on the north. Many buildings were found to be
in good condition and very worthy of being saved. Vacant
land, run-down buildings, too many streets and alleys, and
high-tax delinquency were discovered as pressing problems to the neighborhood and to the city.

No one in the community had privacy; families lived
next to factories, and factories and garages were trying to
operate in blocks which were residential. Definitely something is wrong in any mixture of homes and industry; such
widely diversified activities should not be carried on in the
same area. But it was the opinion of the members of the
planning board that if this mess could be unscrambled, the
industries, businesses, and community residents could
make valuable contributions to the city's financial, economic, and cultural life, as they had in the past.

The next problem discovered in the research study
was that of through streets used by trucks and autos to get
to other parts of the city through the community. While it
takes a great deal of study to know how much traffic exists,
where it originates, and its destination, and while the planning board depended on city agencies for information of

this kind, the basic problem of proper streets is a fairly simple one.

Chicago was planned for horses and buggies rather than for fast-moving motor traffic. It has a north-and-south street every 225 feet, and an east-and-west street every 750 feet, with a "major" street every mile. However, the major streets are not wide enough to accommodate the large numbers of passenger cars and trucks, so most people use any street that is straight and will lead them to their destinations. This results in the use of most of the small side streets in the community by trucks and passenger cars to get from one part of the city to another.

In its report, the planning board made recommendations as to a proper street pattern. They stated that there must be a few special, wide, major streets or highways which people can use if they want to go a long distance at a fairly fast rate of speed. There should also be a few secondary streets which the residents of the community could use to get out of the neighborhood to reach the major thoroughfares. All the other streets should be local streets, designed so they don't go anywhere except from a person's front door—whether it be the front door of the house, the business, the school, or the church—to a secondary street, and then on to the major highways. They should be designed so that through drivers will not want to use them, but delivery trucks and fire engines can do so, and the residents can get to church, school, the library, the park, or the local grocery store.

Consequently, the planning board adopted the following planning principles:

1. The total separation of three kinds of land use:
   a. Residential (including schools, churches, parks, community centers, and local neighborhood retail stores)

    b. The Halsted-Roosevelt community shop-
ping center (this plan was abandoned because of the strategy by the city administration to use this land for the new University
of Illinois Circle Campus)

    c. The industrial and commercial areas

2. The use of the two new superhighways as buffers
between industry and homes and a widening of
14th and 15th streets with the same purpose on
the south

3. The largest possible acreage for residential use,
as is in keeping with the efficient industrial use of
the railroads on the east and south borders of the
area

4. The closing of as many through streets as possible without interrupting the flow of necessary
crosstown traffic

A tentative overall plan was proposed by the planning
board based on the findings of the various community studies and planning principles just described. While this tentative plan was based on a great many facts and very careful
planning considerations, while it represented concerted
time and effort on the part of the planning board, to turn
the proposals into reality would require the cooperation of
the Chicago Planning Commission, numerous city departments, and the local political officials. During this period
the Chicago Planning Commission was also studying the
entire West Central area, and was preparing recommendations, many of which were expected to agree with those of
the Near West Side Planning Board. On points of disagree-
ments, conferences were planned between the two organizations.

In 1952, the planning board expected to concentrate
its efforts on the problems of where major conservation

should be started, in addition to the already existing conservation block, and where new buildings of different kinds
should start. The board had been considering: (1) the vacant land in the area, where new buildings could be built
immediately; (2) residential structures which were sound,
according to various studies, and which should be retained
in the area while some of the unsound structures were
replaced; (3) owner-occupancy, important because it represented a special interest in promoting the growth of the
community and also local financial equity, which could be
a resource in the process of rebuilding.

It was considered probable at that time that the part of
the industrial area east of Halsted Street which is between
Polk Street and Roosevelt Road would be the first to be
considered for industrial development, because this area
contained much vacant land, though few residential dwellings, and because some tentative plans already existed under the auspices of the Western Society of Engineers.

The Chicago Planning Commission had approved the
principle of Land Clearance Commission activity in an area
for proposed industrial development, and the Land Clearance Commission was interested in that particular area. On
the vacant land near the South Water Market, the beginnings of redevelopment of the market could be started
as soon as a study of its problems and needs had been
made.

In the residential area, public housing is usually the
first and last to be redeveloped; the Jane Addams Houses
and the Robert Brooks Homes were last because they were
built in 1937 and 1941 respectively. On the other hand,
Loomis Courts, a relocation project south of Medill School,
was already under construction, and plans were on the
draftingboard for the extension of the Robert Brooks
Homes over most of the remaining area bounded by Racine, 15th Street, the alley behind Ashland Avenue, and the
alley behind Roosevelt Road.

In the rest of the residential area, the planning board was attempting to determine, among other things, the locations of good and bad structures, owner occupancy, and vacant land, so that it could be decided which whole blocks could be conserved, which whole blocks were beyond recall, and where, within other blocks, some new building might be constructed on vacant land while some conservation would be retained.

In deciding on the types of new building to be encouraged, the planning board was thinking in terms of local facts and basic principles. One fact is that "used" or "second-hand" housing is in some ways cheaper than new housing, and that the only way to meet the requirements of all income groups is to include in the supply some used housing.

On the basis of these and other considerations, the planning board adopted the principles of providing in their plan: (1) conservation of existing housing where economically feasible; (2) conversion to housing of some of the structurally sound nonresidential buildings; (3) provision for various kinds of new buildings—single family dwellings, two- and three-flat buildings, and multi-family structures.

In an attempt to determine what funds might be available for these projects, the planning board examined the redevelopment which had already taken place at this time. Congress Street was being built with city, county, and state highway funds. The Central National Bank was rebuilt with private funds controlled by an individual corporation. The funds for repair of individual homes were provided in the small amounts required by the home owners themselves, some coming from savings, others from government insured loans. Funds for Loomis Courts were city and state funds, and those for the addition to Robert Brooks were mostly federal, both coming through the Chicago Housing Authority. The planning board presented these examples to illustrate, as a matter of principle and practicality, that all kinds of funds may be available, and that they must be sought from all sources.

In the following years the Near West Side Planning Board's ever-increasing activity caused it, in 1951, to establish its own office separate from the West Side Community Committee. But as in the case of the parent organization, the driving thought behind the planning board was that a local community, even though composed of groups of many different racial backgrounds and a wide variety of interests, can, through democratic processes, determine for itself the kind of community it should be and how it can be improved; that, working with other local and with appropriate city agencies, it can plan its own redevelopment in a pattern consistent with a citywide planning program; and that through the progressive realization of such a plan, a newly revitalized community can be established.

CITIZEN PARTICIPATION

In the process of getting things done, the people of the community learned first-hand how governmental, political, economic, and social machinery operate and they became more articulate and able citizens. Racial, ethnic, and religious fears were replaced with understanding of common problems. By participating in reforming the physical environment, local people, including local agency and business leaders, learned the relationship of physical factors to their other problems and were thus helped to see how these other problems might be solved. The work of the planning board, different from but fundamental to that of business, religious, educational, and social agencies in the community, created a new frame of reference within which these other agencies became more effective in their particular programs.

In 1954, at the end of six years of work, the planning board had developed general plans for its area with concrete proposals for a series of treatment measures and for priorities. These plans were generally understood by the people and were generally acceptable to the various city agencies concerned with their execution. Some of the treatment was well underway at that time.

The acceptance and support of the work of the Near West Side Planning Board by business and commerce was sufficiently widespread to be a threat to the participation of the little people who lived in the community, who might be stifled by the greater articulateness of business executives and others. In order to keep in balance the growing ability to understand and participate by different types of representatives, the Wieboldt Foundation was appealed to for special funds for the Citizen-education-citizen-participation phase of the program. A three-year grant of $7,500 a year was made by the Wiebolt Foundation in 1952. With this money a general interpretive and educational program was successfully carried out.

Also in 1952 new plans were made for broadening the base of industrial and business participation and support, which took the form of a working arrangement with the West Central Planning Association, whose board of directors was made up of industrial executives. On May 20, 1954, there was a merger of the Near West Side Planning Board with the West Central Association, which paid $600 per month to the planning board for a director's services. This was done to revitalize the association's program so that it could accomplish in the balance of the West Central community the kind of planning being done in the Near West Side Area.

The association committed itself to completing the work of the planning board in its smaller area and to inaugurating the same type of work in the larger five-square mile area known as the West Central community. It also specifically committed itself to active citizen participation both in the Near West Side Planning Board area and in the larger area being started by a widely representative Urban

Renewal Advisory Panel. After the merger in 1954, the reorganized West Central Planning Association, whose membership numbered nearly 100 business and industrial executives, began taking leadership but provided for local participation through cooperation with the planning board, certain other community councils, and the organization of a community advisory panel.

However, the cultivation of active and enlightened citizen participation, essential to successful completion of the work, is always more difficult and expensive than the cultivation of enlightened business leadership. There are more people, they are closer to the realities of life, and they customarily have less control over the myriad factors which daily affect their lives and livelihood. Even when the physical aspect of work of a planning board is well advanced, the field of general citizen participation and education is fairly well covered, the enlightened business and industrial participation in and support of this kind of community program is increasingly well organized, and official city and federal participation is imminent, there is nevertheless the constant danger that the people may be left out.

Certain specific services were required by the 17,000 people within the area covered by the Near West Side Planning Board and the West Side Community Committee. For these requirements of the local population depended on the entire program in the larger area, which included 165,000 people. A demonstration in the selected planning board area was required to point the way to an equally essential and equally effective program in the larger area. During the six years of the Near West Side Planning Board, a few residents of the area consistently participated in deliberations and decisions, hundreds of people participated to a lesser extent, and hundreds more were made aware of and were affected by the work of the board.

With the treatment phase of planning actively under way, the next order of business was to develop in individual families their roles in the ongoing physical changes. In attempting to accomplish this, the planning board community organization technician worked diligently on a block organization among families living east of Halsted Street in the area rezoned upon its recommendation for industry and where, consequently, demolition was impending. Plans were made to clear a blighted area near Hull House through the Land Clearance Commission and to provide housing by private developments for the people to be dispossessed.

It had been suggested by the planning board that while Chicago was giving very special attention to the threatened neighborhood of Hyde Park-Kenwood, where resources of all kinds were tremendous and where if it couldn't be done there, it couldn't be done anywhere, it should give the same kind of special attention to the completely worn-out West Central area, where for many years problems had been insurmountable, where resources of all kinds were limited, and where if it *could* be done there it *could* be done anywhere.

In fact, in 1953 James W. Follin, director of the Division of Slum Clearance and Urban Redevelopment in the federal government, told the planning board that their work in the area during the previous six years was in line with the federal administration's proposal for urban renewal legislation, and that there were strong possibilities that the Near West Side would be designated as one of the two pilot demonstration areas in Chicago.

The result of this was the decision early in 1954 by the Mayor's Housing and Redevelopment Coordinator that the West Central Community Program should be made one of Chicago's pilot urban renewal programs, with official and coordinated city agency leadership and federal participation. Chicago's "Workable Programs," the approval of which had to precede any federal grants, went to Washington. In 1955 further planning was taken over by the Community Conservation Board of Chicago, and various proposals were formulated.

CITY HALL INTERVENTION

By this time, however, the state of Illinois and the city of Chicago were negotiating for a site for the new University of Illinois campus. Various areas of the city were being considered and, since some communities objected to having the campus in their area, its location became a controversial issue.

One of the sites recommended was the eastern end of our neighborhood; but our people strongly opposed it, for we would have had to abandon a large part of our earlier plan (the conservation and rehabilitating of many sturdy two- and three-story brick buildings). We had been assured by city officials that the eastern end of the area was designated for this purpose and, as a result of those assurances, some improvements were underway. Holy Guardian Angel Church, for example, had constructed a new $600,000 church and school in the very heart of the area now proposed for demolition to clear land for the new campus.

To say the least, our residents were greatly disturbed. The whole concept of democratic planning was going down the drain. Everyone felt doublecrossed by city hall clout. For about a year, as the final decision hung in the balance, we were all very pessimistic. When city hall finally made the irrevocable announcement, there was no escaping the fact that we had been sold out. Everyone lost hope. Apathy set in. Public hearings were held, but to no avail. Florence Scala, a long time leader in Hull House and an activist for the rights of the people, was an outspoken foe of the project. She was articulate and militant, but the forces of city hall were overpowering. We lost the battle.

Finally, at a hearing on May 16, 1956, the new area was

designated and the die was cast. We now had a new "conservation area," including essentially our old Near West Side community minus the area east of Halsted and some sections east of Racine Avenue.

This decision had an injurious impact on the Near West Side Planning Board. The leadership became disillusioned, funds became even more difficult to raise, and the board lost much of its effectiveness. However, its research, surveys, and planning were valuable resources for the new city agencies which began to play a more active role in urban renewal.

By 1962 the board was virtually not functioning. However, part of its mission soon became the goal of the Near West Side Conservation Council, a local entity required by the newly established Chicago Department of Urban Renewal, which consolidated the operations of the former Land Conservation Board. Since that time our committee has worked with the local Conservation Council in continued attempts to implement our plan for conservation and redevelopment of the neighborhood.

THE NEAR WEST SIDE TODAY

Since land sales started in 1967, redevelopment and renewal of the community have been progressing rapidly, although it took almost 25 years and $18 million in federal funds. Parcel by parcel the face of the Near West Side has been changing. No longer can the area be labeled a slum. On the east is a huge fortress, the Circle Campus of the University of Illinois; on the west, at Ashland Boulevard, is a new high-rise, Campus Green, with 456 units of luxury apartments. In the heart of the area, around Our Lady of Pompeii Church and Notre Dame Church, is the first of the new housing developments, Westgate Terrace, with 48 townhouses. In other sections, other small units have been constructed or are in process of construction. Many of the old buildings have been renovated, both inside and out, and are even preferred by some people over the newer structures. Home and apartment owners are sandblasting the years of grime off their buildings, exposing the rich, original red of the bricks or white of the limestone. Facades are being restored to how they looked 70 years ago.

The block-long Bishop Street, from Polk to Taylor streets, one of the few tree-lined streets in the neighborhood, has new charm. The maze of rickety fences and gates guarding each front yard has been ripped down, replaced by new lawns and oak trees. Out in the middle of the street is a double cul-de-sac and a center plaza, blocking traffic and creating an ideal spot for children to play street hockey and other games. Half a block north and east, West Polk Street has been closed off with new sidewalks and plantings. It blends nicely with Columbus Plaza, across South Loomis, where a tranquil fountain splashes at the feet of a statue of Columbus. This giant bronze statue by Moses Ezekiel is a momento of Chicago's World Columbian Exposition of 1893. It formerly adorned the Columbus Memorial Building at State and Washington. When the building was razed in 1959, the statue was given to the Municipal Art League and kept in a suburban lumberyard. In 1965, through the joint efforts of the league and the Joint Civic Committee of Italian-Americans, funds were raised, and the Chicago Park District agreed to place the statue on a permanent pedestal and plaza in Vernon Park. Since Victor A. Arrigo, the state legislator, played a prominent role in this project, the Joint Civic Committee of Italian-Americans requested that this park be renamed the Arrigo Park.

The plaza forms a gateway from Vernon Park, leading two blocks east to Mother Cabrini Hospital. South and west of the park a few dilapidated buildings remain, but most have been torn down. In their place are entire blocks of vacant land waiting to be acquired for new townhouses and apartment complexes.

The Jane Addams Houses provide housing for approximately 3,600 persons out of a total population of 28,000 in the area. But very few of these federal homes are occupied by persons who were residents of the community in 1950. By 1960 the population in the Jane Addams Housing Project and the Robert Brooks Homes had become predominantly black.

Nearby, on Taylor Street, the atmosphere changes: here are Italian restaurants and stores that specialize in Italian cheeses, olive oil, salami and other Italian cold meats, anchovies, spices, tomato paste, spaghetti, wine, pastries, a wide variety of fruits and vegetables, meats and other spiced foods required by the Italian palate. The peddlers who once pushed carts or drove horses are now motorized, but the fresh fruits and vegetables, a passion with Italians, continue to be sold. Occasionally a group of men will be seen playing with their bocci balls (a type of lawn bowling) on an empty lot, but the new bookstores catering to the university students are an entirely new phenomenon. And everywhere, over-running the neighborhood are cars, cars, cars, most of which belong to those university students, who commute daily. Here is a clash between the life-style of the new and old residents.

Along Halsted north of Harrison Street are stores and shops that appeal to other population groups, primarily Mexican and Greek. Rice, chile, and tamales stand out as the ingredients of the Mexican diet, and lamb appears to be the most popular Greek item, as evidenced by many butcher shops that specialize in lamb.

A few Greek coffeehouses remain here, remnants of many such establishments that about 30 years ago constituted the social centers for Greek men. Sipping a strong black coffee, smoking their Oriental waterpipes, and engaging in gossip and repartee, the Greek men of the district made these coffeehouses literally their second homes. But with the movement of the Greek community to other sections of the city, these old-world institutions lost their importance. During the past decade, however, about half-a-dozen new Greek restaurants opened for business, providing increasingly popular Greek dishes—and belly dancers.

Another major development was the establishment in 1972 of a new $8 million shopping center at Racine and Harrison, adjoining the northeastern section of the Italian neighborhood and the Chicago Circle Campus. The new, enclosed buildings house a complex of services, 38 shops, and office space for professional people.

On nearby Jackson Boulevard and Loomis Street, the board of education recently constructed the $20 million Whitney Young High School. Known as a "magnet school," it draws students from all over the city.

The corner of Halsted and Polk Streets, famous for over half a century as the site of Hull House, has also changed drastically. Gone are the 13 buildings which once comprised the settlement house and the hundreds of two-flats where people lived. Gone also is Holy Guardian Angel Church, which was constructed at a cost of $600,000 in 1960 and a few years later was demolished because the land was needed for the new university. All that remains on the corner of Halsted and Polk streets is the original Hull House residence, now designated a national historic site, surrounded by the university's fortresslike structures of steel and cement.

So ends the story of the redevelopment of our neighborhood. As in most ventures in life, one does not succeed 100 percent. The efforts which we undertook after World War II yielded many results. We met with some failures, but we also achieved many of our objectives. Others are still to be attained; but by the late 1970s the renaissance of the Near West Side should be complete. It will never again be the ethnic neighborhood described in the first two chapters of this book.

Perhaps the old neighborhood was dying anyway, and something had to take its place. On the whole, I believe we preserved much of the old while adding much that is modern and fresh.

Chapter 9

SURVIVAL AMID CHANGE

THE NEAR WEST SIDE COMMUNITY COMMITTEE TODAY

It is encouraging to us and to our friends that our enterprise continues to exist and after 43 years is still thriving. (The West Side Community Committee was organized in 1938 and incorporated in 1939. However, the Chicago Area Project launched community work in our area in 1934. Thus, combining the early efforts and the actual years of operation of the WSCC, we can say that our enterprise is 43 years old. In 1960 the committee decided that it would be appropriate to change the name to the Near West Side Community Committee.) We have thus disproved the charge of certain cynics that this was another "fly by night outfit." We have weathered many storms, but we have continued to carry on a variety of programs for the prevention of delinquency and the treatment of delinquents.

This cannot be said of the two other community committees first started by the Chicago Area Project in the early

1930s. The North Side Civic Committee, in a predominantly Sicilian neighborhood north of the Loop, and the Russell Square Community Committee, in the predominantly Polish area near the South Chicago steel mills, disbanded over ten years ago. The maintenance and operation of viable community committees no longer was feasible, given the drastic social changes that took place.

On the near north side the Italians were displaced by the Cabrini-Green Housing Project, which is now predominantly black. For about two years the North Side Civic Committee operated in an area about one-half mile north of the old neighborhood, but gradually this area greatly deteriorated and eventually most of the residents were displaced by blacks. The Area Project, with state personnel, organized the North Central Community Committee in the Cabrini-Green Housing Project in the early 1950s, and it functioned fairly effectively until five years ago. When the state worker was withdrawn because of budget cuts, the work of this committee suffered and its program, now carried on by a handful of volunteers, is extremely limited. (A community worker was recently assigned to this area, and this committee is now operating again.)

Russell Square also underwent a population change. As the Polish residents moved out, Spanish-speaking people moved in. Part of this area is now covered by the Mexican Community Committee, another Area Project unit.

In the early 1940s the project also started the first community committee in a black community on the south side. It functioned effectively under the leadership of Golden B. Darby and Mrs. Warren B. Douglas (now Mrs. Sadie Jones), but it too was disbanded after about 20 years. Here again population changes, problems of internal leadership, and departure from the original principles led to dissolution of the South Side Community Committee. However, in this instance two new and effective enterprises were organized: the Beatrice Caffrey Youth Service, organized by Mrs. Jones in the Grand Boulevard area, and the Big Buddies Youth Services, Inc., organized by Alexander McDade in the Grand Crossing-Woodlawn area.

These are only some examples of the problems in maintaining community organizations in urban areas. Is this a defect or limitation of Area Project principles? I think not. Similar changes and difficulties appear in the work of traditional groupwork agencies, many of which have had to abandon their programs or merge with other agencies because of disruptions and dislocations in the inner city areas.

Our enterprise today includes the Near West Side Community Committee, the central body of the organization. It has a membership of several hundred persons who elect the board of 45 directors, who in turn choose 5 additional board members. This board meets officially once a month, but special meetings are called as needed. Composed almost entirely of residents of our neighborhood, along with a few former residents, the board functions not unlike any other board of directors; it discusses neighborhood problems, sets goals, plans programs, formulates policies, raises funds, and, in short, concerns itself with all the affairs appropriate to this general function. By the very nature of its work, it must have a limited number of persons.

In addition to our board of directors, we used to have an active advisory committee composed of executives representing firms and industries located in or near our community. Since many industries have moved out of the area, this committee has become inactive. This group used to offer advice and served as another means of establishing contacts with the wider community. It conducted a finance campaign among friends and local industries, and it aided us with other resources from time to time. For example, a member of this advisory committee contributed a $3,000 filtering plant for the swimming pool at Pompeii Camp, and another member enlisted the services of an architect for a nominal fee to draw up the plans for these swimming facilities.

Recently our committee decided to establish a new advisory committee composed of former members who no longer reside on the Near West Side but who are successful business and professional men. Periodic meetings with this group enables our commitee to receive advice and assistance from persons who have a broad background of experience—and the get-togethers provide an opportunity for reunions with old-timers.

Our central group, however, extends itself in various other ways. There are standing committees, which include board members or other residents, and special committees, which are appointed from time to time to deal with special projects. Beyond this inner structure are numerous local clubs, churches, organizations, societies, and other neighborhood groups which have collaborated with us in many ways. In addition, hundreds of people contribute financially either directly or by attending dances, banquets, carnivals, or picnics—all of which are means of raising funds.

This enterprise is not easy to maintain. It requires endless attention, and we must use all available means to get people to come to meetings and participate in activities. Personal contacts are the best technique for attracting attention, and community newsletters, bulletins, and brochures have also been effective devices for enlisting people. But we are not always able to counteract some of the forces in urban life that prevent neighborhood organization. People move around, both geographically and socially, and as a result we lose members. This exodus greatly increased with urban renewal, new expressways, and Circle Campus; but new members come in as old ones move out.

We believe that our former members are better citizens for their having participated in our group. Many of these people show an active interest in the affairs of their new neighborhoods and at times take the leadership in similar ventures. We are often called by former residents to assist in organizing in their new areas.

Today our committee operates with a cash budget of about $15,000 a year, half of which is made available by the Chicago Area Project from funds it receives from the Community Fund of Chicago. Eighteen other community committees in the city are affiliated with the project and receive similar financial assistance. Our share of the budget is raised through benefits, contributions from local merchants, and other special events.

Community committees can operate on limited budgets because of the unique way they and the Chicago Area Project can secure outside resources. The state of Illinois through its Commission on Deliquency Prevention, provides the personnel for our work. A community worker recruits and trains volunteers, directs programs, and in other ways assists in the administration of the whole operation. However, recently the community worker was assigned to another district; hence the committee has operated for over a year without a worker. The new commission has agreed to provide another indigenous worker in the very near future. In addition, we have assigned to our organization a community representative from the local Urban Progress Center, a federally funded agency launched by President Johnson as part of the War on Poverty.

Also operating out of our office is a representative from Project Find, a federally sponsored program for senior citizens. This worker visits the homes of elderly residents or interviews them at our office and explains and interprets various social welfare services, assists them in making application for welfare benefits, or refers them to appropriate agencies or resources.

In the early days we had assigned to us workers from other state and federal agencies. Our committee also employs some part-time program workers occasionally. If we were to calculate the salaries of the workers made available to us from government sources in addition to our cash budget, the overall cost would amount to approximately $50,000 a year. Other resources not included in this figure are the volunteer services of many residents and contributions in kind which run into thousands of dollars.

Whenever we identify a problem which needs our attention we either try to organize a program in our own name, or we establish a new organizational form to deal with it. As already mentioned, when we started a health and sanitation program by distributing 4,000 garbage receptacles, we organized a "coordinating council" on a ward-wide basis. In relation to the housing problem we put together the Near West Side Planning Board. A more recent example was the credit union; our officers saw the need for such a financial resource and organized a separate corporation for this purpose. The credit union has 200 members and assets of $25,000. As goals are achieved or conditions change, these special organizations are usually phased out.

CHALLENGE AND RESPONSE

Difficulties of the Committee

We never regarded our venture as a cure-all for local problems. But we were firmly convinced that any solution of community problems should significantly include the people who are daily confronted by those problems. We have found abundant human resources in the community, but we would be wrong to deny we've had difficulties.

Our committee is not set up to compete with any other institution. However, we do have a vital stake in the work local institutions carry on. For this reason we feel we should collaborate with them to help them increase their effectiveness in meeting the needs of our people. This has not always been an easy task. There have been school administrators who did not want the participation of our people in the affairs of the school, regarding this as an invasion of their sphere of influence or authority. The offer by a local group to aid one settlement house financially was rejected because the head resident felt the people might begin to make demands and interfere with the management of the institution.

We recall our boldness in requesting equal representation on the board of trustees of another settlement. Since the board of this settlement—as true of practically all of them—was composed exclusively of persons residing outside our community, we proposed that it add to its board an equal number of representatives from our community.

Our audacity, of course, had reverberations. People began to ask, "Who controls this group of upstarts?" After all, had the settlement ever done anything that was not in the best interests of our people? Possibly not, but that, of course, was not the issue. "These many years," we said in essence, "you have aided us and helped us become Americanized and paved the way for our participation in a society based on democratic principles. Well, now we are without doubt thinking and behaving as Americans, and what's more we want to assume our responsibilities as citizens. We believe it is only fitting and proper therefore that we participate significantly in the management of this institution." Subtly, but unmistakably, we were reminded that he who pays the piper calls the tune.

There have been other points of disagreement and at times conflict with church leaders, politicians, and other neighborhood leaders, but all in all, we have done remarkably well, we believe, in working with our local institutions on common matters affecting the welfare of our children, young people, and adults.

Developing working relationships with our parish churches, social settlements, community centers, public parks, and many other public and private agencies in and outside our area thus continues to be a major effort of our committee. Perhaps the most important of these relationships today is with the city's Department of Urban Renewal, since we are still in the process of redeveloping the neighborhood, and with the University of Illinois, Circle Campus, which plays an extremely important role in the community.

A few years ago another citizens' group was established to deal with social problems of the area immediately south of the neighborhood described in this book. Known as COUP—Community of United People—it concerns itself largely with the needs of over 40,000 black and Latin residents in this low-income community. Another community organization immediately west of our area is the West Side Organization. Established in 1964, its purpose is to develop leadership and to promote welfare programs.

As in all good causes, however, there are often unexpected consequences which give rise to new problems. The most vexing of these problems today is the problem created by the over 20,000 students now attending the university. Although the university has constructed some parking facilities, they are not adequate. As a result, students park all over the neighborhood, depriving residents of their spaces. It must be remembered that our neighborhood consisted of two- and three-story buildings on 25-foot lots; there was not always enough space for garages or parking lots, so many residents park on the street in front of their buildings. Nowadays there is fierce competition for parking space, especially during the day, when the students are in school. This has greatly irritated people in the community, and the committee is constantly discussing the issue with university officials.

Some residents became so angry when students parked illegally on private property that they took matters into their own hands. They raised over $400, hired brick-layers, and walled in a car with cement blocks. This event made the front pages of the newspapers, and of course the police came to investigate. The irony was that this particular car did not belong to a student. It had been stolen and was abandoned there. But the residents had made their point, and they hoped that students, and university officials, too, would take heed—or else.

Still, the University of Illinois has influenced many of our young people to attend college. It has provided new jobs for local residents, and some university facilities have been made available for meetings, recreation, and educational purposes.

The Ethnic Problem

Over the years the Near West Side Community Committee has cooperated with citywide organizations whose purposes have been to improve the status of Americans of Italian extraction, to fight discrimination, and to open new doors to opportunities in business, politics, and in the professions. It was natural that our committee align itself with such organizations, since the Near West Side has been and continues to be one of the few remaining Italian ethnic neighborhoods in the city. From 1945 to 1954 the committee collaborated with the Italian Welfare Council, which also made available financial assistance for our community work. When this council disbanded, the Joint Civic Committee of Italian-Americans, a new organization, continued to give leadership to Italian-American community action programs, especially in relation to antidefamation measures.

Among key leaders who organized and developed this enterprise are Vincent E. Ferrara, Joseph Barbera (now both deceased); Anthony Paterno, Congressman Frank Annunzio, Peter R. Scalise, Victor J. Failla, Dr. Mario O. Rubinelli, Anthony Bottalla, Dr. James F. Greco, and many others. Among the men now giving leadership to this ethnic program are Charles C. Porcelli, Anthony J. Fornelli, and James Coli.

As I described in earlier chapters, our Italian people in the early days of immigration were victims of discrimination. Today the types of incidents I referred to are much less frequent. Currently it is likely to be the blacks and Spanish-speaking people who are victims of gross discrimination.

However, there are still other types of prejudice which continue to affect the Italian-American people and hinder their development. The practice of the mass media, for example, in constantly using the terms "Mafia" and "Cosa Nostra" affects many Italian people on the Near West Side and throughout the city. The influence may be subtle or indirect, but it is there. A few years ago the television series *The Untouchables* dramatized the exploits of organized crime almost every week, portraying the gangsters as Italian. Italian names were used almost exclusively, and invariably a common setting for the gangsters was an Italian restaurant or pizzeria. Today we have the *The Godfather* and other movies which portray Sicilians and Italians in violent, criminal roles. Newspapers, magazine articles, and books on the "Mafia" continue to flourish.

Thus the evil deeds of a few distort the picture of the Italian people as a whole, and this image especially places obstacles to the upward mobility of men and women who aspire to higher positions in business, the professions, and politics but are the victims of guilt by association.

I have known many people of Italian ancestry who were denied important positions in business and government because of their ethnic background. Today they are proportionately under-represented in the executive suites of business; rarely is an Italian placed on the county or state slate of either political party, though in Illinois there are over a million people of Italian ancestry. Justification does exist for the objections raised by Italian-American leaders that they are sometimes maligned, defamed, and discriminated against by the Anglo-Saxon establishment.

Because Italian leaders have felt this injustice and prejudice, they banded together in the Joint Civic Committee of Italian-Americans. Still active today, they are also focusing attention on a related, even broader issue: ethnicity and ethnic identity. Joining forces with Polish, Jewish, and other ethnic groups, they are promoting social, educational, and cultural programs to present the positive contributions of ethnic groups to American life. Like ours, their goals are to open new doors of opportunity, enhance their status, and achieve greater representation and participation in all institutions of our society. In the achievement of some of these goals the JCCIA is also cooperating with the National Center for Urban Ethnic and Neighborhood Affairs in Washington, D.C., under the leadership of Mgsr. Gino Baroni and Rev. Paul Asciola.

Opposition to the Chicago Area Project

It is a little-known fact that Saul Alinsky began his career with Clifford Shaw and the Chicago Area Project. In the early 1930s, Shaw assigned to Alinsky, then a young sociologist at the Institute for Juvenile Research, the task of launching a self-help community organization which soon became known as the Back-of-the-Yards Neighborhood Council. But because of differences in ideology and possible personality differences, Alinsky, who was very ambitious, broke off with Shaw and started his own organization, the Industrial Areas Foundation.

Shaw's idea of grassroots democracy was to organize

community committees open to and representative of the rank-and-file citizens of the neighborhood. Shaw felt that the residents could accomplish much to improve the neighborhood by working cooperatively and in collaboration with all the social groupings and institutions of the area. In other words, he envisioned everyone working together on a mutual basis. Through informal groups in which the ordinary citizen would be free to participate, everyone would have a direct voice in the affairs of the organization and derive whatever prestige or recognition would be accorded. But while Alinsky perhaps agreed with all this philosophically, he proceeded in ways which ran counter to Shaw's conception of how people should work.

Shaw's model was perhaps based on his conception of how people in the rural community in which he grew up banded together as neighbors to build a new barn when one burned down, or aided a family in distress, or accepted troubled persons as human beings. To Alinsky apparently this model was not realistic in the context of the urban neighborhood. Accordingly to Alinsky, effective social action is possible only by the coalition of power groups in the community. It would then be the leaders of the power groups who would negotiate, and at times threaten, the establishment.

These differences aside, the point here is that the notion of embarking into the community and mobilizing local leaders for youth welfare work and delinquency prevention measures started with Shaw, and the Back-of-the-Yards Neighborhood Council originated through the Chicago Area Project. After a few years, Alinsky left the Back-of-the-Yards and launched similar ventures in other cities; in the 1960s he organized The Woodlawn Organization (TWO) on the South Side of Chicago. The Back-of-the-Yards Neighborhood Council under the leadership of Joseph Meeghan continues today as a viable enterprise for community action on youth problems. While its structure is somewhat different from a community committee, its approach is similar.

Although the Chicago Area Project has had a partnership relationship with the state of Illinois for 43 years, the relationship has not always been harmonious. Over the years, even recently, there have been administrators in the different state agencies which have furnished the personnel for this work, who have questioned this arrangement and have tried to curtail or restructure the operation in such a way as to change the methods which we have employed.

An issue in this regard was recently resolved by the members and leaders of the Chicago Area Project and the community committees by their collective power; they bombarded the governor's office and their legislators with thousands of letters and had a show-down. The legislators, who strongly support the Area Project, held up the budget of the Department of Corrections until assurances were given and our demands were met.

However, opposition to the work of the Area Project continued, and early in 1975 a statewide campaign was launched to introduce legislation to establish this community program as a separate state agency. These efforts succeeded, and in September, Governor Dan Walker signed the measure to create the Commission on Delinquency Prevention, which became operational on January 1, 1976.

Variations of the earlier criticism of the CAP continued later by the Welfare Council of Metropolitan Chicago (now the Council for Community Services). The project was often asked to indicate its criteria for establishing new community committees. Our answer was simply that we gave priority to areas of high rates of delinquency and that communities became eligible for Area Project assistance when there was evidence of a local group capable and willing to undertake the organization of a community committee. The only limitation to the scope of its service was the availability of personnel and funds.

Since more and more of the staff members who joined the Area Project were college graduates, criticisms of untrained workers became rare. But a similar criticism questioned the qualifications of workers with delinquent and disturbed children. Our answer was that Area Project members were selected for their capabilities in stimulating and encouraging participation in the local committee, assisting these organizations in planning and carrying on their programs, and developing opportunities for contact between delinquent children on the one hand and conventional youth and adult groups on the other. It was pointed out that our workers were not psychologists, caseworkers, or counselors. However, when staff encountered emotionally disturbed individuals who required the aid of such professionals, it was the policy of the Area Project to refer them to the psychological clinic at the Institute for Juvenile Research or similar agencies.

In the light of the goals which we have been discussing in this book, namely, to deal with the child through people with whom he is in natural and spontaneous contact, the Area Project seeks to achieve the rehabilitation of the child as well as the prevention of delinquency through the indispensable human resources to be found in the community. Hence, the principal device required for this is community organization. The persons employed in Area Project work are selected for their skills in securing entree into such circles and in providing a type of leadership which results in the establishment of local institutions concerned with the welfare of youth.

Still other questions raised by the council were concerned about the ethnic and racial composition of local community committees. It was sometimes pointed out that most of the committees were composed predominantly of one nationality or racial group. Reference has already been made to the fact that the fundamental procedure of the Area Project entails the use of the spontaneous or "natural" social groupings as an instrumentality for effecting delinquency prevention purposes. If there is any validity in this procedure it follows that the groups with whom such work is carried on are as accepted as the conditions under which they exist. Among these conditions is the fact that associations, loyalties, and identifications tend to follow ethnic and racial lines.

The spontaneous and natural groupings in the city are usually, though not always, coterminous with ethnic and racial groupings. Again usually, though not invariably, natural physical neighborhoods tend to be populated by homogeneous subgroups. As a result, local community committees tend to be made up of a particular ethnic or racial group and function largely within them.

The policy of the Area Project is to stimulate the development of local delinquency prevention groups through which access may be had to the world of the child. Thus, even in neighborhoods in which a number of such subgroups may exist side by side, it is necessary to encourage the development of community committees, each of which may function in terms of prevailing lines of social contact within each group. It would follow from this that in adjacent neighborhoods comprising a variety of subgroups, under prevailing patterns of association children of each group would characteristically be accessible to the influence of adults within their own group. By the same token, where there existed a neighborhood in which a number of subgroups were integrated into a single structure of association and contact, the local community committee would be required to reflect this integration in the composition of its governing board.

The widespread tendency to regard residents of low-income areas with suspicion and to question their talents and capacities has resulted in some attempts to bring the control of the programs of community committees under a central board. Such an arrangement would negate the basic principles of the Chicago Area Project. Fortunately, the board of the CAP has always avoided this traditional administrative pattern. However, there are times when some board members express dissatisfaction with the limitations on their power of decision. Newcomers to the board feel they do not perform a meaningful role; but after serving a number of years, they grasp the spirit of the Area Project and become staunch supporters.

Another problem common to enterprises operating with democratic principles is the extent of participation in action programs. Without exception, in the organizations encouraged by the Area Project an effort has been made to encourage the widest possible participation. But in several cases the organizations, though operating for several years, ceased because the original leadership was in one clique or faction in the community, though even in these cases new committees with a broader base were established later.

Another possible problem is the domination or exploitation of the organization by a small group of ambitious people or perhaps even by an aggressive member of the staff. Although the work may suffer temporarily, democratic processes set to work by the residents usually solve the problem.

Notwithstanding these and many other problems, no doubt found in other welfare organizations also, there is reason to believe that one of the most effective ways to help people in local areas is to aid and encourage them to assume every possible responsibility for the administration, control, and operation of the welfare activities in their community. Local communities will, of course, need the services of governmental and voluntary agencies to help solve many of their problems. But the value of such services is increased if they are not superimposed but come through local residents.

PROBLEMS OF EVALUATION

The effectiveness of the type of program developed by the Area Project should, of course, be appraised. As Helen Witmer and Edith Tufts point out in their evaluation of delinquency prevention programs in the United States, there are many problems with this.[47] Even relatively reliable data are difficult to secure, and it is virtually impossible to ascertain the relationship between trends and specific programs. Conscientious attempts to secure reliable data with reference to Area Project programs have not furnished results which will stand up under rigorous scientific scrutiny.

For example, before it could be stated unequivocally that a program had been successful in preventing delinquency it would be necessary to establish that there was a differential downward trend in rates of delinquency in the experimental areas over against the control area; that the program was responsible, and not the records; and that the changes were permanent and not cyclical. Finally, it would have to be determined whether or not, quite apart from the major purposes, the indirect and associated accomplishments justified the expenditure in time and money. This is important, for it is quite possible that these values furnish adequate justification for our work quite apart from our success with delinquents.

On the other hand, before it could be established that a program was an absolute failure, it would be necessary to establish that the method had been put into operation conscientiously, that it had been applied over an area large enough to furnish a basis for a final conclusion, and that it had been in operation long enough for an adequate trial.

In several communities where a program has been in operation for a number of years there has been a downward trend in the volume of delinquency. The difficulty is in interpreting what this trend means, because data fluctuate widely in small areas and even if it can be established that a decrease has taken place, it may have been due to other influences in the community or to changes in administrative procedure.

There are other ways, however, of appraising the value of local neighborhood programs. When the people of a neighborhood band together and work collectively in a community welfare program, new and basic resources are tapped. As residents work on behalf of their children and community, new positive attitudes are a result. This means, therefore, that the child is living in a new situation and responding to new, constructive social influences. It seems reasonable to assume that these influences and the improvements in general living conditions which the residents are able to effect operate both for the prevention of delinquency and the treatment of delinquents. If just one child is helped to stay out of trouble and go straight, a verifiable accomplishment has been made.

It should be stressed that methods employed not only in our work but in all welfare programs should be re-examined and critically evaluated from time to time. Without continuous experimentation and testing, new methods of treatment and prevention are not likely to be developed.

In view of these considerations, it seems probable that at this time the results of the evaluation must be on terms of encouraging or discouraging trends, or in gains in knowledge or in values which have accrued in the work of the project. On this basis, and from my 40 years of experience, I make three positive statements based on the progress in those communities where the method was wholeheartedly or conscientiously put into operation: (1) The development of stable and vital citizens' organizations in low-income areas is feasible. (2) Community committees and affiliated citizen groups perform many varied and useful functions. (3) Community committees have attacked the problem of delinquency directly as well as by attempting to improve the community.

Feasibility

The development of citizen organizations in low-income areas to assume responsibility for planning and operating a wide variety of constructive community enterprises is entirely feasible. Whenever the Area Project has consistently and unreservedly sought to aid in the formation of such groups, they have developed and have become constructive forces in the life of the community. In the areas in which we work, these groups have taken the form of community committees, civic committees on youth, and subcommittees which include within their memberships representatives of all ages, occupations, and social strata.

Except in rare instances, it has been demonstrated that these community committees have vitality and stability. Despite changing membership and the usual clashing of personalities and interests, they have persisted through the years with increasing strength and determination. Where they have had complete and unquestioned responsibility and control, they have managed their budgets and applied their talents and energies to their avowed purpose as scrupulously and effectively as any of the recognized agencies in the welfare field in Chicago.

The evidence supporting these assertions is to be found in the history of the community committees themselves. Their activities are a matter of record; and since they are currently in operation, any questions about what they are and what they are not can be cleared up by personal visits or investigations.

Functions

The functions which these community committees have rendered in their communities are many and varied. Examples of the many types of activities in which they have engaged were described in the account of the work of the Near West Side Community Committee and in the references of other citizens' groups already described in this chapter.

The Problem of Delinquency

Although many examples were given in this book on how community committees deal with the problem of delinquency, I believe it is appropriate in this context to summarize the methods utilized—methods which our experience has shown are based on a sound understanding of the problem.

In the first place, the civic activity of residents is in itself the beginning of the modification of the character of the community. The new attitudes formed among adults as a result of participation in a communal welfare program create a new situation and a new set of social influences for the child. And apart from these more subtle influences are the actual facilities which the communities are able to make available to their children, and the improvements in general living conditions which they are able to effect. These improvements in the community operate both for prevention of delinquency and the treatment of delinquents.

The second method of treatment involves the attempts of the local committees to deal more directly with the delinquent or his group, through persons who have participated in, or at least are familiar with, the activities, plans, and aspirations of the delinquent. All methods of dealing directly with the delinquent by correctional agencies have serious limitations, but these are reduced to a minimum by using persons who have some experiential basis for the understanding of the delinquent rather than persons who are separate from him by a gulf created by cultural differences or professional standards.

Finally, the community committees are able to assist in the rehabilitation of adult and young offenders by incorporating them into active roles in the committee or some branch of its work. By this method the parolee or ex-offender is actively reincorporated into a conventional group; his role in the community is redefined, which results, in turn, in a redefinition of his own conception of himself. The vigor with which parolees and others with criminal records have worked to improve their own communities and keep boys out of delinquency has been one of the most encouraging aspects of this method.

INFLUENCE OF THE AREA PROJECT

Shaw fully realized the importance of social movements and reforms which would in time, perhaps, improve conditions in disadvantaged communities. But he regarded these efforts as segmental and long range, leaving untouched the immediate basic community conditions. For this reason he worked fervently for over 25 years to develop the Chicago Area Project, which he firmly believed was formulated on principles which were logically sound and consistent with democratic practice and humanitarian values.

Clifford Shaw's death in August 1957 meant the loss of an irreplaceable leader. However, he left a legacy of ideas and practices which serve to inspire his associates and the thousands of residents and workers in local communities throughout the nation. The Chicago Area Project, therefore, continues as a truly fitting living memorial to an outstanding social scientist, a humanitarian and a great leader of a significant social movement.

Clifford Shaw's studies and the Chicago Area Project have undoubtedly had a constructive impact on welfare work generally. Witness, for example, the many new community and neighborhood programs which have been launched since 1950 with the slogans, "reaching the un-reached," "hard to reach youth projects," and similar types of programs which stress using the constructive resources of the community. Speaking on the subject "Delinquents: Outcasts of Society," Bertram Beck said in 1954:

> I find it rather odd to be speaking on this topic in Chicago, for it was in this city some thirty years ago that Clifford Shaw and his associates embarked on their series of studies that dramatically illustrated the manner in which we failed to reach delinquent children and their families, and served as the basis of one of the most significant experiments in reaching the unreached that continues to this day. Clifford Shaw's early works were not well received by the social work profession. Perhaps it was that we, as a young profession, were overly sensitive to criticism and he, as a stalwart enthusiast, was less than delicate. Or perhaps it was that he like all men of rare ability, was ahead of his time.[48]

To a remarkable degree, Shaw's hopes and objectives have been achieved. This is readily apparent as one looks at the broad spectrum of human services now being delivered and promoted. The Area Project was initially severely criticized, but today its emphasis on local leadership and management is reflected even in the activities of its harshest critics. In many ways the Area Project has affected the programs of local policy-making institutions and group-work agencies. Some institutions have created departments to reduce the cleavage between themselves and the community, while others have developed neighborhood centers and have started to employ more neighborhood workers and group leaders.

Some of the programs based on Area Project procedures have surpassed the project in terms of size, popularity, and even achievements. Many private social agencies throughout the country have embarked on programs to "reach the unreached," using indigenous workers now referred to as "paraprofessionals." Social agencies now seek to include local residents on their board of directors. Federally funded national programs stipulate that the poor must be represented on community action projects.

The Area Project has urged and continues to urge a principle now being embraced more and more by administrators in the criminal justice system, that if campaigns against crime are to be successful, everyone must participate. Enlightened officials in this field are beginning to admit that the old techniques have not worked.

Donald Santarelli, former administrator of the United States Law Enforcement Assistance Administration (LEAA), recently told Carl Rowan, "You can add cops, judges, prosecutors, and hardware until the Treasury is emptied, but you'll never reduce crime much until you get the people involved."

Perhaps we can conclude that Clifford Shaw was a half-century ahead of his time.

POSTSCRIPT

At the beginning of my career, my assignment with the state's Children's Leisure Time Service as a gang worker lasted less than a year. The state terminated this project as federal funds became available and the WPA was established. Since my sister was working, I did not qualify for WPA. However, the Chicago Area Project had funds available to enable me to continue working in the neighborhood with the newly launched program. Since this work was primarily in the afternoons and evenings, I was able to attend college in the mornings.

My salary in those days came from a special fund available to the Chicago Area Project from the Boy Scouts of America, and the source of those funds was royalties from Irving Berlin's song "God Bless America," earmarked to promote scouting in "less chance areas." I was a pioneer in that recruiting and training program, which started around 1935 and continues to this day as "street-corner scouting."

I attended junior college for two years, then went to Lewis Institute, now merged with the Illinois Institute of Technology, graduating in 1938 with a B.S. degree. Later I studied sociology at the University of Chicago. Upon graduating from college I passed a civil service exam and became certified as a junior research sociologist in the Department of Sociology of the Institute for Juvenile Research, of which Clifford Shaw was departmental head. Prior to this I had received my naturalization papers in order to qualify.

As a staff member of the Institute for Juvenile Research, I worked on the Near West Side until 1945, when I was given responsibilities in other parts of the city. But I continued in contact with the West Side Community Committee. From 1954 to 1957 I served as Clifford Shaw's administrative assistant and had central office responsibilities for the Area Project, which by that time had a total of 12 projects throughout the city. At the same time I assisted Mr. Shaw in teaching several courses on delinquency at the Downtown College of the University of Chicago. I now teach these courses at DePaul University.

When Clifford Shaw died in August 1957, I succeeded him as administrative director of the Chicago Area Project. At about the same time a reorganization of welfare services by the state of Illinois transferred the community services phase of the institute, which was the Area Project, into the Illinois Youth Commission. I became assistant superintendent for Cook County of this new agency. We continued to expand delinquency prevention work based on the methods of the Area Project. On January, 1 1976, I was appointed by Governor Dan Walker as the first executive director of the newly established Commission on Delinquency Prevention. In this capacity I now have responsibilities for promoting statewide projects.

In 1939, with a secure job and my career showing some promise, Ann Sodaro and I were married. We lived on the

Near West Side for about ten years. Within five years we had three children: Robert, Patricia, and Dolores, now all married. We have three grandchildren. In 1957 we moved to Hinsdale, a suburb of Chicago, where we live today.

These many years have seen changes in the life of the immigrant boy who landed here in 1919 with fear and trepidation. He moved along with some anxieties but never in a spirit of resignation; and finally he achieved a satisfying and significant place in society. Also during these four decades the problems of an ethnic community were confronted with daring and determination to make it a better community.

Backing up all these efforts, both in the life of that boy and in the history of the community was the Chicago Area Project, the creation of Clifford R. Shaw, a social scientist and a humanitarian in the best sense of the word.

When I was growing up, my mother would often proudly tell me that when I was born the Italian flag was raised on one of my father's small boats in the harbor in Marsala, Sicily. This was done so that as he came home from Malta—on the schooner *El Niobe,* in which he had part interest with an uncle—he would know that the child they were expecting was a boy.

The birth of a boy was especially welcomed and celebrated with greater joy and clamor than if the child was a girl. The first bath water, when a boy was born, would be thrown out the balcony into the street to symbolize that this boy's place would eventually be in the world. But the first bath water of a baby girl would be flushed down the latrine, symbolizing, I hope, nothing worse than the fact that this poor female child's place would eventually be in the home.

My mother made a big point about the flag being raised to announce my birth. To her this had special significance; it was an omen that I would eventually grow up to be someone of importance. That never really happened, but perhaps in some way we cannot understand, this incident was the beginning of what Eric Berne calls the "script" of a life. Perhaps this explains the ambitiousness and exuberance people have attributed to me ever since I was a child.

NOTES

INTRODUCTION

1. Public Law 93-415, 93rd Congress, Sept. 7, 1974, p.1. "The Congress finds that—(1) juveniles account for almost half the arrests for serious crimes in the United States today."
2. Nelli, Humbert. *The Italians in Chicago, 1880–1930.* Used an early draft of this book.
3. Southside Community Committee. *Bright Shadows in Bronzetown.* Chicago: Chicago Area Project, 1949.
4. Short, James F., Jr. Introduction, Clifford R. Shaw and Henry D. McKay, *Juvenile Delinquency and Urban Areas.* Chicago: University of Chicago Press, 1969. p. xlvi.
5. Snodgrass, Jon. *The American Criminological Tradition;* and "Clifford Shaw and Henry McKay: Chicago Criminologists," *British Journal of Criminology,* scheduled for publication in 1976.
    One of the many errors in Snodgrass's account is that he treats the Area Project by means of a few essays written about it mostly in the early days rather than by means of empirical investigation. There is reason to believe that theory was altered in practice.
6. Fish, John Hall. *Black Power/White Control,* pp. 111, 97.

257

7. Rivera, Ramon J., and King, Richard M. "Toward Decentralization: A Strategy for Establishing Juvenile Court Branches in Cook County." Berwyn, Ill.: MacNeal Memorial Hospital, March, 1974, p.54.

8. Lombroso, Cesare. Quoted in Marvin E. Wolfgang, "Pioneers in Criminology," pp. 369–70.

9. Addams, Jane. *Twenty Years at Hull House*, chapter 6.

10. Platt, Anthony. *The Child-Savers*, p. 79.

11. Murphy, Patrick. *Our Kindly Parent . . . The State*, p.172.

12. Hart, Sara L. *The Pleasure Is Mine*, chapter 11.

13. Shaw, Clifford R.; Zorbaugh, Frederick M.; McKay, Henry D.; and Cottrell, Leonard S. *Delinquency Areas*, p. ix.

14. *Ibid.*, p. 199.

15. Southside Community Committee, pp. 101–102.

16. Short, p. liii.
    Short's essay should be consulted for a fuller treatment of the sociological theory behind the practice of the Area Project.

17. Snodgrass, *American Criminological Tradition*, p. 139.

18. Wood, Elizabeth. In Studs Terkel, *Hard Times*, p. 437.

19. Snodgrass, *American Criminological Tradition*, p. 140.

20. Terkel, p. 351.

21. Alinsky, Saul. *Reveille for Radicals*, p. 81.

22. Terkel, p. 353.

23. Sanders, Marion K. *The Professional Radical: Conversations with Saul Alinsky*. New York: Harper & Row, 1970, p. 19.

24. Alinsky, p. 83.

25. *Ibid.*, p. 82.

26. Alinsky, Saul. Quoted in Fish, pp. 28–29.

27. Short, p. xlii.

28. Murphy, p. 14.

29. See also Richette, Lisa Aversa. *The Throwaway Children.*

30. Morris, Norval. *The Future of Imprisonment*, p. 29.

31. See Morris, Norval, and Hawkins, Gordon. *The Honest Politician's Guide to Crime Control.*

32. Finestone, Harold. "The Chicago Area Project in Theory and Practice." In Irving A. Spergel, *Community Organization*, p. 186.

33. See Terkel, Studs. *Division Street: America*, especially the first and last selections in the book.

34. See Stott, William. *Documentary Expression and Thirties America.* New York: Oxford University Press, 1973.
    Stott's treatment of personal documents in sociology, especially Shaw's use of them, is not adequate.

35. Becker, Howard S. Introduction to Clifford Shaw, *The Jack-Roller*. Becker has discerned four continuing functions for life histories: communication between members of different social classes, presentation of the continuities of underlying processes, innovation in research, and evaluation by employing a life history as a touchstone for judging a theory.

36. Two exceptions are "The Life Histories of W. I. Thomas and Robert E. Park," ed. Paul J. Baker.

37. For a treatment of such movements between worlds see my *Genius: An Art of Making New Worlds* (unpublished dissertation, University of Chicago, 1972). This form of genius would be to true genius what the "psychopathology of everyday life" is to true psychopathology.

38. See Dawley, David. *A Nation of Lords;* and Keiser, R. Lincoln. *The Vice Lords.*

CHAPTER 3

39. Taylor, Hasseltine Byrd. *The Chicago Area Project as Seen by a Social Worker.* Unpublished document in author's possession, 1935.

40. _____. *Report on the Investigation of the Area Project.* Unpublished document in author's possession. 1935.

41. O'Brien, Howard Vincent. "All Things Considered." *Chicago Daily News,* Nov. 4, 1940.

42. Martin, John Bartlow. "A New Attack on Delinquency," pp. 507–508.

CHAPTER 4

43. Cohen, Albert. *Delinquent Boys,* p. 28.

CHAPTER 6

44. Mason, Thomas P., Jr. "Juvenile Corrections."

45. Shaw, Clifford. *The Natural History of a Delinquent Career.*

46. Finestone, Harold. "Reformation and Recidivism among Italian and Polish Criminal Offenders."

Chapter 9

47. Witmer, Helen L., and Tufts, Edith. *The Effectiveness of Delinquency Prevention Programs.*
48. Beck, Bertram. Remarks at a meeting of the Welfare Council of Metropolitan Chicago, April 5, 1954.

BIBLIOGRAPHY

Abrahamson, Julia. *A Neighborhood Finds Itself.* New York: Harper and Brothers, 1959.

Addams, Jane. *Twenty Years at Hull House.* New York: Macmillan, 1910.

_____. *Second Twenty Years at Hull House.* New York: Macmillan, 1930.

Alinsky, Saul. *Reville for Radicals.* Chicago: University of Chicago Press, 1945.

_____. *Rules for Radicals.* New York: Random House, 1971.

Baker, Paul J. "The Life Histories of W. I. Thomas and Robert E. Park." *American Journal of Sociology* 79: No.2. Sept. 1974, 243–60.

Beck, Bertram. "Delinquents—Outcasts of Society." Lecture delivered in Chicago: Welfare Council of Metropolitan Chicago, 1955.

_____. "Innovations in Combatting Juvenile Delinquency." *Children,* March–April, 1965, 69–74.

Bennett, James R. "Genius: An Art of Making New Worlds." Ph.D. dissertation, University of Chicago, 1972.

Bernstein, Saul. *Youth on the Streets.* New York: Association Press, 1964.

Biddle, William W., and Biddle, Loureide J. *Encouraging Community Development: A Training Guide for Local Workers.* New York: Holt, Rinehart, and Winston, 1968.

Burgess, Ernest W. "Community Organization—a Resource for Youth." In *The Delinquent and His Neighbors,* ed. Anthony Sorrentino. Milburn, New Jersey: R. F. Publishing, 1975.

Carney, Frank J.; Mattick, Hans W.; and Callaway, John D. *Action on The Streets: A Handbook for Inner City Youth Work.* New York: Association Press, 1969.

Carr, Lowell Julliard. *Delinquency Control.* New York: Harper and Brothers, 1940.

Cavan, Ruth Shonle. *Juvenile Delinquency.* Philadelphia: J. B. Lippincott, 1962.

Clinard, Marshall B. *Slums and Community Development.* New York: The Free Press, 1966.

————. *Sociology of Deviant Behavior.* New York: Holt, Rinehart, and Winston, 1974.

Cloward, Richard A., and Ohlin, Lloyd E. *Delinquency and Opportunity.* Glencoe, Ill.: The Free Press, 1960.

Cohen, Albert K. *Delinquent Boys: The Culture of The Gang.* Glencoe, Ill.: The Free Press, 1955.

Coleman, James S. *Community Conflict.* New York: Free Press of Glencoe, 1957.

Dawley, David. *A Nation of Lords: The Autobiography of the Vice Lords.* New York: Anchor Books, 1973.

De Young, Henry G. "The Near West Side Story." *The Chicagoan.* January, 1974.

Finestone, Harold. "Reformation and Recidivism Among Italian and Polish Criminal Offenders." *The American Journal of Sociology,* Vol. 72. No. 6, May 1967, 575–88.

————. The Chicago Area Project In Theory and Practice." In *Community Organization,* ed. Irving A. Spergel. Beverly Hills: Sage Publications, 1972.

Fish, John Hall. *Black Power/ White Control.* Princeton: Princeton University Press, 1973.

Gans, Herbert J. *The Urban Villagers.* Glencoe, Ill.: The Free Press, 1962.

Glueck, Sheldon, ed. *The Problem of Delinquency.* Boston: Houghton Mifflin, 1959.

Hart, Sara L. *The Pleasure is Mine: An Autobiography.* Chicago: Valentine-Newman, 1947.

Hayes, Wayland J. *The Small Community Looks Ahead.* New York: Harcourt, Brace, 1949.

Hughes, Helen MacGill., ed. *The Fantastic Lodge.* Boston: Houghton Mifflin, 1961.

Johnson, Elmer Hubert. *Crime, Correction and Society.* Homewood, Ill.: Dorsey Press, 1964.

Keiser, Lincoln R. *The Vice Lords: Warriors of the Street.* New York: Holt, Rinehart, and Winston, 1969.

Klein, Malcolm W., and Myerhoff, Barbara, eds. *Juvenile Gangs in Context: Research and Action.* Los Angeles: Conference Report: Youth Studies Center, University of Southern California, 1963.

Knapp, Daniel, and Polk. Kenneth, "The Ideological Roots of the New Constituency Leadership," Chapter 3 in *Scouting The War on Poverty.* Lexington, Massachusetts: Heath Lexington Books, 1975.

Kobrin, Solomon. "The Conflict of Values In Delinquency Areas." *American Sociological Review* 16: October, 1951, 653–661.

_____. "The Chicago Area Project—A 25 Year Assessment." *The Annals of American Academy of Political and Social Science,* March, 1959:19–29.

_____. "The Formal Logical Properties of the Shaw-McKay Delinquency Theory." In *Ecology, Crime and Delinquency,* ed. Harwin L. Voss and David M. Petersen. New York: Appleton-Century-Crofts, 1971.

Kobrin, Solomon; Puntil, Joseph; and Peluso, Emil. "Sociological Aspects of the Development of A Street Corner Group: An Exploratory Study." *The American Journal of Orthopsychiatry* 32 (October, 1961):685–702.

_____. "The Impact of Cultural Factors on Selected Problems of Adolescent Development in the Middle and Lower Class." *The American Journal of Orthopsychiatry* 36 (April, 1962):387–390.

_____. "Criteria of Status Among Street Groups." *Journal of Research in Crime and Delinquency,* January, 1967, 98–118.

McKay, Henry D. "The Neighborhood and Child Conduct." Philadelphia: *The Annals of American Academy of Political and Social Science* 261 (January 1949):32–41.

_____. "Differential Association and Crime Prevention: Problems of Utilization." *Social Problems* 8 (Summer, 1960):25–38.

_____. "Social Influence on Adolescent Behavior." *The Journal of the American Medical Association* 182 (Nov. 10, 1962):643–649.

_____. "Report on the Criminal Careers of Male Delinquents in Chicago." *Task Force Report: Juvenile Delinquency and Youth Crime.* The President's Commission on Law Enforcement and Administration of Justice. U.S. Government Printing Office, Washington, D.C., 1967. 107–114.

_____. *Subsequent Arrests, Convictions, and Commitments Among Former Juvenile Delinquents.* Submitted to the President's Commission on Law Enforcement and Administration of Justice, 1967. (Copies available through Anthony Sorrentino, Chicago Area Project, 160 N. LaSalle Street, Chicago, Illinois 60602.)

MacIver, Robert M. *The Prevention and Control of Delinquency.* New York: Atherton Press, 1967.

Martin, John Bartlow. "A New Attack on Delinquency." *Harper's Magazine,* May, 1944.

Mason, Thomas P., Jr. "Juvenile Corrections: Five Issues To Be Faced." In *Popular Government,* Institute of Government, The University of North Carolina at Chapel Hill, May 1971.

Matza, David. *Delinquency and Drift.* New York: Wiley and Sons, 1964.

Miller, Walter B. "Lower Class Culture as a Generating Milieu of Gang Delinquency." *Journal of Social Issues* 14: (April, 1958), 5–19.

Morris, Norval. *The Future of Imprisonment.* Chicago: University of Chicago Press, 1974.

Morris, Norval, and Hawkins, Gordon. *The Honest Politician's Guide to Crime Control.* Chicago: University of Chicago Press, 1970.

Morris, Terence. *The Criminal Area.* London: Routledge and Kegan Paul, 1957.

Murphy, Patrick. *Our Kindly Parent . . . The State.* New York: Viking, 1974.

Nelli, Humbert. *The Italians in Chicago, 1880–1930.* New York: Oxford University Press, 1970.

O'Brien, Howard V. *All Things Considered* Chicago Daily News, Nov. 4, 1940.

Park, Robert E., and Burgess, Ernest W. *Introduction to The Science of Sociology.* Chicago: University of Chicago Press, 1921.

Plant, James S. *Personality and the Cultural Pattern.* New York: The Commonwealth Fund, 1937.

Platt, Anthony. *The Child-Savers: The Invention of Delinquency.* Chicago: University of Chicago Press, 1969.

Poston, Richard W. *Democracy Is You.* New York: Harper & Brothers, 1954.

Rice, Stuart A. "Hypothesis and Verification in Clifford R. Shaw's Studies of Juvenile Delinquency." *Methods in Social Science,* ed. Stuart A. Rice. Chicago: University of Chicago Press, 1931. 549–565.

Richette, Lisa Aversa. *The Throwaway Children.* New York: Dell, 1969.

Sanders, Marion K. *The Professional Radical: Conversations with Saul Alinsky.* New York: Harper and Row, 1970.

Shaw, Clifford R. *The Natural History of a Delinquent Career.* Chicago: University of Chicago Press, 1931.

————. "Housing and Delinquency." In *Housing and the Community,* report prepared by the Committee on Housing and Delinquency of the President's Conference on Home Building and Home Ownership, 1932.

———. *The Jack-Roller.* Chicago: University of Chicago Press, 1930, Rev. ed. 1966.

Shaw, Clifford R.; Burgess, Ernest W.; and Lohman, Joseph D. "The Chicago Area Project." In *Coping With Crime.* New York: Year Book of the National Probation Association, 1937.

Shaw, Clifford R., and Jacobs, Jesse A. "The Chicago Area Project: An Experimental Community Program for the Prevention of Delinquency in Chicago." In *Proceedings of the 69th Annual Conference of the American Prison Association.* New York: 1939.

———. "The Chicago Area Project." In *Criminal Behavior,* ed. Walter C. Reckless. New York: McGraw-Hill, 1940. pp. 508–516.

Shaw, Clifford R., and McKay, Henry D. *Social Factors in Delinquency.* No. 13, Vol. II, Report on the Causes of Crime. National Commission on Law Observance and Enforcement, U. S. Government Printing Office, Washington, D.C., 1931.

———. *Juvenile Delinquency and Urban Areas.* Chicago: University of Chicago Press, 1942, Rev. ed. 1969.

Shaw, Clifford R.; McKay, Henry D.; and McDonald, James F., *Brothers in Crime.* Chicago: University of Chicago Press, 1938.

Shaw, Clifford R., and Myers, Earl D. "The Juvenile Delinquent." Chapter 14 of *The Illinois Crime Survey.* Chicago: The Illinois Association for Criminal Justice, 1929, pp. 645–761.

Shaw, Clifford R., and Sorrentino, Anthony. "Is Gang Busting Wise?" *National Parent Teacher.* (January, 1956):8–20.

Shaw, Clifford R.; Zorbaugh, Frederick M.; McKay, Henry D.; and Cottrell, Leonard S. *Delinquency Areas.* Chicago: University of Chicago Press, 1929.

Short, James F. ed. *The Social Fabric of the Metropolis.* Chicago: University of Chicago Press, 1971.

———. ed. *Delinquency, Crime and Society.* Chicago: University of Chicago Press, 1976.

Short, James F., and Strodbeck, Fred L. *Group Process and Gang Delinquency.* Chicago: University of Chicago Press, 1966.

Snodgrass, Jon. "The American Criminological Tradition: Portraits of the Men and Ideology in a Discipline." Ph.D. dissertation, University of Pennsylvania, 1972.

———. "Clifford Shaw and Henry McKay: Chicago Criminologists," *British Journal of Criminology,* scheduled for publication in 1976.

Sorrentino, Anthony. "The Chicago Area Project After 25 Years." *Federal Probation,* 23: June, 1959:40–45.

———. "Cultural Aspects of Violent and Disturbed Youth." In *Proceed-*

ings of the Ninetieth Annual Congress of Correction. New York: American Correctional Congress, August 1960: 437–451.

———. *The Delinquent and His Neighbors.* Milburn, New Jersey: R. F. Publishing, 1976.

South Side Community Committee. *Bright Shadows in Bronzetown.* Chicago: South Side Community Committee, 1949.

Spergel, Irving A. *Community Problem Solving: The Delinquency Example.* Chicago: University of Chicago Press, 1969.

———. *Racketville, Slumtown, Haulburg.* Chicago: University of Chicago Press, 1964.

———. *Street Gang Work: Theory and Practice.* Reading, Mass.: Addison-Wesley, 1966.

———, ed. *Community Organization: Studies in Constraint.* Beverly Hills: Sage Publications, 1972.

Stott, William. *Documentary Expression and Thirties America.* New York: Oxford University Press, 1973.

Suttles, Gerald D. *The Social Order of the Slum.* Chicago: University of Chicago Press, 1968.

Tannenbaum, Frank. *Crime and the Community* Boston: Ginn, 1938.

Task Force Report: *Juvenile Delinquency and Youth Crime.* The President's Commission on Law Enforcement and Administration of Justice. U.S. Government Printing Office, Washington, D.C., 1967.

Taylor, Hasseltine B. *The Chicago Area Project as Seen by a Social Worker.* Unpublished document in author's possession. 1935.

———. *Report on the Investigation of the Area Project.* Unpublished document in author's possession. 1935.

Terkel, Studs. *Division Street: America.* New York: Avon Books, 1967.

———. *Hard Times.* New York: Pantheon, 1970.

Thrasher, Frederic M. *The Gang.* Chicago: University of Chicago Press, 1927.

Tunley, Roul. *Kids, Crime and Chaos.* New York: Harper and Brothers, 1962.

Whyte, William Foote. *Street Corner Society.* Chicago: University of Chicago Press, 1958.

Wilensky, Harold L., and Lebeaux, Charles N. *Industrial Society and Social Welfare.* New York: Russell Sage Foundation, 1958.

Witmer, Helen L., ed. "The Prevention of Juvenile Delinquency." Philadelphia: *The Annals of the American Academy of Political and Social Science,* 322 (March, 1959).

Witmer, Helen L., and Tufts, Edith. "The Effectiveness of Delinquency Prevention Programs." Washington, D.C. U.S. Department of Health, Education and Welfare, Children's Bureau Publication No. 350, 1954.

Wolfgang, Marvin E. "Pioneers in Criminology: Cesare Lombroso (1835–1909)." *The Journal of Criminal Law, Criminology and Police Science.* 52: No. 4, 361–91.

Wolfgang, Marvin E.; Savitz, Leonard; and Johnston, Norman, eds. *The Sociology of Crime and Delinquency.* New York: John Wiley, 1962.

Zorbaugh, Harvey Warren. *The Gold Coast and the Slum.* Chicago: University of Chicago Press, 1944.

INDEX